John Healy

Ancient Irish Church

John Healy

Ancient Irish Church

ISBN/EAN: 9783744730570

Printed in Europe, USA, Canada, Australia, Japan

Cover: Foto ©Lupo / pixelio.de

More available books at **www.hansebooks.com**

Sixpence Monthly. One Penny Weekly.

THE BOY'S OWN PAPER.

"The BOY'S OWN PAPER has had a greater success than any other boys' paper of a high class published in England, and the healthy vigour and excellence of its stories, to say nothing of the instructiveness of its articles, are a model of what a boy's periodical ought to be."—*The Fortnightly Review.*

"It appeals directly to every youth, whether he loves fiction or field sports, and has a charm even for boys of a maturer age."—*Daily Telegraph.*

"A very feast of good things."—*Christian.*

"A perfect storehouse of amusement and instruction."—*Saturday Review.*

"As for the tales, they tell of travel, sport, and adventure all over the world. Games of all kinds are discussed with the careful attention they deserve. Science and the severer pursuits are by no means neglected."—*Times.*

"A wonderful sixpennyworth."—*Queen.*

"Full of the kind of reading in which boys most delight."—*School Guardian.*

"Simply splendid."—*Western Press.*

"Those parents who desire that their sons shall grow up into brave, manly, and cheerful young men, should certainly give them the BOY'S OWN PAPER. Almost everything to delight the heart of an English boy can be found in its pages."—*English Churchman.*

"Of the BOY'S OWN PAPER it is safe to say that it would have earned the blessing of Dr. Arnold of Rugby, whose ideal of periodical literature it realises by its treatment of a wide diversity of themes, secular as well as religious, in a truly Christian spirit."—*Christian Leader.*

"Presents in pleasant and playful, though very varying form, all that is manly, brave, honourable, and therefore deserving of imitation by the growing generation of boys."—*Pall Mall Gazette.*

THE BOY'S OWN ANNUAL.

832 pages. With 14 Coloured or Tinted Plates and upwards of 500 Wood Engravings.

8s. in Handsome Cloth.

PUBLISHED AT 56, PATERNOSTER ROW, LONDON,
And Sold by all Booksellers.

THE BOY'S • OWN • BOOKSHELF.

ADVENTURES OF A THREE-GUINEA WATCH. By Talbot B. Reed. 3s. 6d.

FOOTBALL. A Popular Handbook of the Game. Including Practical Instructions by Dr. Irvine, C. W. Alcock, etc. 1s. 6d.

CRICKET. A Popular Handbook of the Game, with Practical Instructions. By Dr. W. G. Grace, Rev. J. Pycroft, Lord Charles Russell, Frederick Gale, and others. 2s.

A GREAT MISTAKE. A Tale of Adventure. By T. S. Millington. 3s. 6d.

THE FIFTH FORM AT ST. DOMINIC'S. A School Story. By Talbot B. Reed. 5s.

THROUGH FIRE AND THROUGH WATER. A Story of Adventure and Peril. By T. S. Millington. 3s. 6d.

HAROLD, THE BOY-EARL. A Story of Old England. By J. F. Hodgetts. 3s. 6d.

INDOOR GAMES AND RECREATIONS. Edited by G. A. Hutchison. Illustrated with numerous Engravings. 4to, gilt edges. 8s.

OUTDOOR GAMES AND RECREATIONS. Edited by G. A. Hutchison. 8s.

MY FRIEND SMITH. By Talbot Baines Reed. 5s.

THE WIRE AND THE WAVE; or, Cable-Laying in the Coral Seas. A Tale of the Submarine Telegraph. By L. Munro. 3s. 6d.

OUR HOME IN THE SILVER WEST. A Story of Struggle and Adventures. By Gordon Stables, M.D., R.N. 3s. 6d.

Published at 56, Paternoster Row, London;
And Sold by all Booksellers.

THE
ANCIENT IRISH CHURCH

THE
ANCIENT IRISH CHURCH

JOHN HEALY, LL.D.

RECTOR OF KELLS

London

THE RELIGIOUS TRACT SOCIETY

56, PATERNOSTER ROW; 65, ST. PAUL'S CHURCHYARD
AND 164, PICCADILLY
1892

CONTENTS.

	PAGE
INTRODUCTION	7

CHAPTER I.
Early Christianity 11

CHAPTER II.
The Arrival of Saint Patrick 17

CHAPTER III.
Missionary Labours of Saint Patrick . . . 26

CHAPTER IV.
Character of the Ancient Irish Church . . . 38

CHAPTER V.
Saint Columba 52

CHAPTER VI.
Saint Columbanus 70

CHAPTER VII.
Ascetics and Anchorites 82

CHAPTER VIII.
The Ministry of Women 89

CHAPTER IX.
Church Officers Peculiar to Ireland . . . 99

CHAPTER X.
SAINT AUGUSTINE OF CANTERBURY AND THE IRISH CHURCH 109

CHAPTER XI.
POINTS OF DIFFERENCE BETWEEN IRELAND AND ROME 115

CHAPTER XII.
CONCLUSION OF THE EASTER CONTROVERSY . . . 126

CHAPTER XIII.
THE EIGHTH CENTURY 130

CHAPTER XIV.
THE DANISH INVASIONS 141

CHAPTER XV.
INFLUENCE OF THE DANISH INVASIONS ON THE CHURCH 148

CHAPTER XVI.
CONVERSION OF THE DANES 156

CHAPTER XVII.
RISE AND PROGRESS OF THE ROMISH PARTY . . . 162

CHAPTER XVIII.
THE SYNOD OF KELLS 176

CHAPTER XIX.
THE ANGLO-NORMAN INVASION. 181

CHAPTER XX.
CONCLUSION 187

INTRODUCTION.

The History of the Ancient Irish Church has an importance of its own. It concerns not merely the Irishman who naturally desires to learn how Christianity came to be preached in his own land, for the subject is of scarcely less interest to the dweller in England or Scotland. The former finds in Ireland the counterpart of the old British Church, and traces to that island, besides, the source whence much of the Christianity of the Anglo-Saxon was first derived. As he marks how from time to time the English Church struggled for liberty —how, long before the time of the Reformation, the authority of the Pope was resisted or rendered only a grudging recognition —he will rightly trace this independent spirit to the tone originally given to the Church by the Celtic missionaries. The latter looks to the Church of Ireland as the parent Church of his own. The story of Iona, and of the conversion of the tribes of Caledonia, is as much Irish as it is Scotch. But to the student of general Church History, Ireland is also important. Just as, in some unfrequented islands, types of animal and vegetable life exist which have become extinct elsewhere, and by study of these we may learn much of the former fauna and flora of places where all the conditions of life have changed; so Ireland retained rites and ceremonies and forms of government long after they had ceased to exist in every other country. In this way we may learn much of the general state of the Church in the fifth century from the state of Ireland as late as the twelfth.

Perhaps the greatest interest of all will be felt by those who, rejoicing in the liberty of a reformed faith and an emancipated Church, will see in Ireland the last of the Western Churches to acknowledge the supremacy of the Pope. When all other parts of Western Europe had already for centuries acknowledged his sway, Ireland was still independent.

In the following short sketch I have endeavoured to present as true a picture as I could make. I have consulted histories written by men of all shades of opinion, but for the facts I have relied almost entirely on the original authorities themselves. Of the Lives of Patrick and the other saints I have made but sparing use. They are too full of the marvellous to be of much value in ascertaining mere sober fact. I have therefore preferred, where possible, the older and more authentic works of Patrick himself.[1] Bede has been largely drawn upon for the incidents of the Irish missions in England. He was devoted to the Roman interest, but he is not unfair to his opponents. Much use has also been made of the works of Giraldus Cambrensis; but he is so prejudiced against everything Irish, and at the same time so credulous, that his work is to be used with caution. The Life of Malachy, who was the great instrument in bringing Ireland under the sway of the Pope, has been written by Bernard of Clairvaux, and I have made much use of it; but the discrepancies between Ber-

---

[1] A convenient edition of these works has lately been issued by the Religious Tract Society.

nard and the Irish Annals are so numerous and important that the two cannot be reconciled; and the latter have seemed to me in general the more worthy of credence, for the simple reason that Bernard's work is written with a purpose, whereas the Annals are pure unadorned records of the events.

The other sources of information are for the most part indicated in the text or the notes.

THE ANCIENT IRISH CHURCH.

CHAPTER I.

EARLY CHRISTIANITY.

Before the close of the fourth century the Christian Church had passed through many vicissitudes and had gained many victories. When the contest began between the small company of believers — despised and persecuted as they were—on the one hand, and the great power of Imperial Rome on the other, few would have ventured to predict that Christianity would ever take the place of paganism as the religion of the multitude; and yet, long before the time of which we write, it had been shown that the weakness of God is stronger than men, and that He in His great providence had chosen the weak things of the world to confound the things that are mighty. As early as the time of Justin Martyr, the Christian apologist could boast that 'there is no race of men, whether of Barbarians or of Greeks, or bearing any other name, either because they live in wagons without fixed habitation, or in tents leading a pastoral life, among whom prayers and thanksgivings are not offered to the Father and Maker of the universe, through the name of the crucified Jesus.' But in the year 400 it needed not that an apologist should direct attention to the fact. The old worships were already for the most part forgotten. The temples of the gods had been destroyed or turned to Christian uses. The spread of Christianity was in some respects a more striking fact then than it is even at the present moment, for the diffusion of knowledge and the discoveries of modern times have revealed to us the existence of millions who have not as yet heard the sound of the Gospel; whereas in that age men's minds never went much beyond those countries which were subject to the imperial power. 'All the world' was to them synonymous with the Roman Empire, and in this sense, 'all the world' was Christian.

This abundant success was not without its serious drawbacks. The converts in the earliest ages were gathered from those whose hearts God had touched, and who, having been brought to a true knowledge of the Saviour, were ready to make any sacrifices and to endure any persecutions for His name's sake. But the case was far different when, after the conversion of Constantine, Christianity became the religion of the State, and multitudes changed their faith without abandoning their superstition. Men who had been taught that they should worship *some* god, but that it mattered little which, might easily become converts; but they were scarcely the class of men who would aid in preserving the purity and zeal of the earlier ages.

Accordingly we find that the fourth century, although it was a time when large numbers were added to the Church, was not an age of real missionary enterprise. Instances are recorded of new Churches having been founded at that period, but none of them owe their origin to the labours of apostles solemnly sent forth for the purpose of evangelization. In the case of Abyssinia, for example, two youths, who had been taken prisoner by the inhabitants, instructed their captors in the faith of Christ, and spread among all the people the light of the Gospel. In Georgia, too, a captive was the first to preach amongst the people the unsearchable riches of Christ, and thus a 'little maid' was honoured of God in being chosen to be the means of their conversion.

The Christian Church, in its corporate capacity, gave no sanction to these and similar enterprises, and had quite forgotten that its mission was to preach the Gospel to every creature. In the apostolic age the idea was that Christianity should be like a great sea, spreading over the whole earth. In the fourth century Christians were content that it should be like a river—a broad and mighty river, it is true, but with heathenism as banks on each side, unmeasured in extent, and not to be reached by the healing waters.

When Christianity became generally diffused over Western Europe, two nations were passed over. The Irish were not evangelized until the fifth century, and the tribes of Germany and the northern parts of the Continent remained in heathenism for some centuries later. Both of these facts have to be kept in mind when we come to study the history of Christianity in Ireland.

The particular time at which a Church was founded must necessarily influence its future to a great extent, particularly when, as in Ireland, the country is more or less isolated from the rest of the world, and is scarcely, if at all, influenced by the intellectual and spiritual movements in other lands. It is thus that the peculiar monastic character of Irish Christianity is to be explained. If it had been founded earlier or later, monasticism might have been introduced, but it would have been different in kind, and would never have become the sole rule of the Church. On the continent of Europe the old monastic ideas soon became antiquated, and new developments so revolutionized the system that it retained in the end no resemblance to the original institution. Ireland continued through many ages to perpetuate that which in other places was only a passing fashion. In many ways too, as we shall see, Ireland retained for centuries the peculiarities of the age in which she first received the faith; and it is this, indeed, that lends particular interest to her history, for in no other country of Europe could we find, even down to the twelfth century, a survival of the peculiar doctrines and usages that existed in the fifth.

The paganism of the German tribes and Norsemen had also its influence on the Irish Church. First of all it afforded scope for missionary enterprise, and provoked enthusiasm and zeal, which were crowned with abundant success, and which must have reacted most beneficially on the Church that sent forth her children to preach the Gospel. In later years the heathen Norsemen, having made settlements on the Irish shores, brought trial and suffering to the Christians, breaking up many of the religious establishments and schools of learning; and at a still later period, when these same Norsemen had been converted to Christianity they had no small share in revolutionizing the Celtic Church and in bringing it into subjection to the see of Rome.

When it is said that Irish Christianity dates from

the fifth century, it is not meant that there were absolutely no Christians in the country before that time. Many reasons, on the contrary, would lead us to believe that some progress in the work of evangelization had already been made. For example, we know that before this time Christianity had obtained a footing in Britain, and there is every reason to believe that a constant intercourse was kept up between her and the neighbouring island. Irish ports, too, were often visited by Roman merchants, and some of these were very probably Christians.

Irishmen, again, were great travellers, and occasionally rose to eminence as bishops and presbyters of the Church in different countries. Mansuetus, first bishop of Toul (A.D. 350), is said to have been Irish, and so also was Celestius, who became one of the chief propagators of the Pelagian heresy. We have not, it is true, any historic record of these Christian Irishmen returning to their own country, or keeping up correspondence with their friends at home; but it is not improbable that some of them did so, and thus introduced the religion which they had learned in a foreign land.

Another probable source of Christian instruction was the number of slaves obtained either by purchase or conquest, sometimes from Britain, and sometimes even from Gaul. Patrick himself was a Christian slave in Ireland long before he thought of visiting the country as a missionary.

These conjectures are borne out by the fact that the ancient legends, however inconsistent they may be in other respects, nearly always agree in stating that a Christian Church existed in the country long before the time of Patrick.

Finally, we have Prosper of Aquitaine telling us

in his *Chronicle*, in a passage quoted afterwards by the Venerable Bede, that Pope Celestine, in the year 431, consecrated one Palladius, and sent him to the Irish believing in Christ as their first bishop. This has been accepted by most historians as proof positive that there were at that time some who had already received the faith.

But when full weight has been given to all these considerations, it will nevertheless appear certain that before the preaching of Patrick the number of Christians in Ireland must have been very small. Prosper speaks in another place of Palladius as 'having made the barbarous island Christian,' from which one would be led to conclude that his mission was that of an evangelist to the heathen rather than that of a bishop for the faithful. But it is very evident that Prosper was only imperfectly acquainted with the facts of the case. For this latter statement he seems to have had no grounds whatever. From Irish sources we learn that Palladius was very far indeed from making the barbarous island Christian; on the contrary, his whole mission was a failure. He landed, it is said, on the coast of Wexford, but found that the 'Irish believing in Christ,' whom he was sent to shepherd, were non-existent; and he met with such determined opposition from the prince of that district that he shortly afterwards re-embarked, and never set foot again on Irish soil. Accordingly, when Patrick, the great apostle of Ireland, entered his missionary labours in the beginning of the fifth century, he found the whole country given over to the superstitions of Druidism. Indeed, Ireland and Scotland and the more remote parts of Brittany were then the only places where that ancient cult survived.

CHAPTER II.

THE ARRIVAL OF SAINT PATRICK.

THE end of the fourth century and beginning of the fifth was a time of trial to the inhabitants of Britain. Under the protection of the Romans they had made considerable progress in civilization and the arts of peace, but they had become quite unused to the science of war. Accordingly, when the Roman legions were withdrawn, the Britons found themselves in a defenceless condition, and exposed to the hostile attacks of those tribes which had never been brought under the imperial yoke. Picts came down from the northern parts of Scotland, Scots crossed over from the coasts of Ireland; they destroyed the villages, plundered the possessions, and sometimes even seized the persons of the more civilized, but less warlike inhabitants of the country from which the protectors had been withdrawn.

In one of these piratical expeditions, a prey of 'many thousand men' was brought across the sea, and placed as slaves among the tribes of Ulster. Among the rest was a young lad of sixteen, son of a deacon and grandson of a priest, who was destined by God to be thus prepared for a great mission, and to be the instrument in His hands of leading a whole nation to the knowledge of the truth. His baptismal name was Succat. He became better known to posterity by his Latin name of Patricius or Patrick.

There have come down to us a hymn in the Irish

language, and two short works in Latin said to have been written by this famous man. In one of these, his *Confession*, he gives a short epitome of his life. In the other, his *Epistle to Coroticus*, he pleads with a Welsh prince for the liberation of some slaves who had been carried into captivity on the very day of their baptism. The Latin of these two documents is rude and archaic. The quotations from Scripture are numerous, and they show that the writer was not acquainted with Jerome's translation, but employed one of those older Latin versions [1] which were in use before the so-called Vulgate had obtained general acceptance. Both these considerations form a strong presumption in favour of the age and authenticity of these writings; and the presumption is further strengthened by the fact that they differ most essentially from the compositions of succeeding centuries, in the entire absence of the miraculous and the marvellous. These works, therefore, must be our principal guide in ascertaining the facts of Patrick's life.

We learn from the *Confession* that the hardships of his captivity were regarded by him as a just punishment for his sins. 'I knew not the true God,' he says, 'and was led away captive into Ireland with many thousand men, according to our deserts; because we had gone back from God, and had not kept His commandments, and were not obedient to our priests, who used to admonish us for our salvation;[2] and the Lord brought upon us the anger of His indignation, and scattered us among many nations, even to the ends of the earth.'

---

[1] For an account of the version used by Patrick and other early Celtic writers, see chapter xiii.

[2] This is curiously like a passage in the Second Epistle of Clement, chap. xvii.

The immediate result on Patrick was to lead him to seek earnestly the grace of God. Day and night he continued instant in prayer, and the answer that came to his soul cannot be better described than in his own words. 'The Lord made me conscious of my unbelief, that all too late I might remember my faults and strengthen my whole heart towards the Lord my God, who had respect to my low estate, and had pity on my youth and ignorance. He kept me before I knew Him, and before I had sense or could distinguish between good and evil, and protected and comforted me, as a father his child. Therefore I cannot, nor indeed ought I to keep silence concerning so great benefits and such great grace bestowed on me in the land of my captivity; for this is the only recompense we can offer, that after God has reproved us or caused us to know our sinfulness, we should exalt and confess His wonders before every nation that is under the whole heaven.'

The history of the Christian Church furnishes us with many examples of what pious slaves can do; but it does not seem to have entered Patrick's mind at this time that as he had received so many blessings from the hand of God, he should endeavour to be a means of blessing to those who were around him. His only thought was of deliverance. Tending the sheep day by day, he was all the time longing for his liberty. After six years of servitude, acting on the impulse of a dream, he fled from his master and made his way to the shore. There he lived for a time in a rude hut which he constructed for himself, but was at length taken on board a vessel, and after some adventures found his way to his father's home in safety. But the freedom he had so earnestly desired did not bring the contentment that he had anticipated. Finding himself once more amongst Christian people, and enjoying the privileges of Christian worship, his thoughts were reverting continually to the people of Ireland, and a great purpose gradually formed itself in his mind : to return to the land of his captivity as a Christian missionary.

While these thoughts were in his heart, and he was pondering whether he should hearken to his relatives and friends, who counselled that as he had gone through so many tribulations he should go nowhere from them; or whether he should follow the dictates of that inward prompting which seemed to urge him forward, towards the great work, a voice seemed to come to him, which said, 'He who gave His life for thee is He who speaks in thee.' On another occasion he saw in a dream one, Victor, coming from Ireland, the bearer of innumerable letters, on one of which was written the words, 'The Voice of the Irish.' In describing this vision, he says, 'While I was reading the beginning of the letter, I thought that I heard in my mind the voice of the men themselves—those who live near the Wood of Foclut, which is beside the Western Sea. And thus they cried, "We pray thee, holy youth, to come and walk amongst us." And I was greatly pricked in my heart, and could not read any more; and so I awoke. Thanks be to God that after many years the Lord has given them the answer to their prayer.'

Notwithstanding these which he regarded as Divine intimations of the great mission which was before him, Patrick remained many years before giving himself up to the work. On every hand he encountered nothing but opposition. The members of his family earnestly besought him to relinquish the idea. They offered him many gifts and entreated him with sorrow and tears. His seniors reasoned with him, and were offended because he would not yield to them. Others were hindering him, and were talking behind his back and saying, 'Why does he run into danger amongst enemies who know not God?' They objected that one rustic in his manners and without proper education was unfit for the work. They even went so far as to bring against him an indiscretion of his boyhood, and to urge that by it he was for ever rendered unfit for the office of a Christian missionary. 'It was on account of the anxiety which it occasioned me,' he says, 'and with a sorrowful mind that I unbosomed myself to my dearest friend, telling him what I had done in my youth in one day, nay, rather, in one hour, because I was not yet able to overcome.' His 'dearest friend' on this occasion betrayed his confidence, hoping by this means to dissuade him from what seemed to be a most hazardous enterprise. So persistent was the opposition with which he was met that many refused to the last to recognise his work. He obtained in the end an abundant reward for his labour—'beautiful and beloved children,' as he puts it, 'brought forth in Christ in such multitudes.' Thus it was shown that his work was the work of God. But not even then did his friends regard his mission with favour. 'Mine own people,' he says regretfully, 'do not acknowledge me: a prophet has no honour in his own country.'

It is not to be wondered at that under such circumstances Patrick hesitated long before taking the decisive step. It was a grief to him in after years that he was so slow in obeying the heavenly call. 'I ought to give thanks to God without ceasing,' he says, 'who often pardoned my uncalled-for folly and negligence, who did not let His anger burn fiercely against me; who allowed me to work with Him, though I did not promptly follow what was shown me, and what the Spirit suggested.'

It is only incidentally that Patrick gives any information as to how he was occupied during this time of waiting. He tells us that he was living with his relatives 'in the Brittanias'[1] at the time when he had the dream about the 'Voice of the Irish.' He seems also to have been with them when his final resolve was taken, for he tells us that in going to Ireland he gave up all the advantages arising from his father's social position. 'My father was a decurio,' he says. 'I do not blush, neither am I sorry that I have bartered my nobility for the good of others.' From this it would appear that most of his time was spent with his family at their home in Britain.

In other places he speaks of his brothers in Gaul, probably using the word brothers in a religious sense, that is to say, members of the same ecclesiastical community. He says that his object in writing the *Confession* is that after his death he might leave it to his brethren in Gaul. And again he tells us that he sometimes earnestly desired to leave his work in Ireland in order that he might 'go as far as Gaul, to visit his brethren and see the face of the saints of the Lord.' The two statements are not incompatible. He may well have spent part of his time

---

[1] The Romans divided England into six provinces, of which two were named Brittania (Prima and Secunda). Brittania Prima was mostly south of the Thames, Brittania Secunda was in the west, and included Wales and some adjoining parts of England. Patrick speaks of his home being in the Brittanias, but gives no more precise information.

in his father's house, and part in one of the monasteries of Gaul, where he would have enjoyed spiritual and educational advantages which could not be had in Britain, owing to the disturbed state of the country and the withdrawal of the Roman legions.

So far we have followed Patrick's own writings, using them the more freely because there is such good reason for believing that the documents are authentic. But when we take up any of the large number of 'Lives of St. Patrick' which have been written, we feel that we are breathing an entirely different atmosphere. In the one case the moderate and unsensational character of the narrative disposes us to accept it as a truthful story. In the other, the preponderance of the miraculous element and the high colouring which manifestly belongs to a later age cause us to pause, and throw a considerable shadow of doubt over the whole account.

The oldest of Patrick's biographies is generally believed to have been composed not much more than a century after his death. Of this Life a manuscript exists, written in the first years of the ninth century, and in it the scribe complains that the copy from which he was transcribing had in many cases become illegible by reason of its age. Documents which can boast such a respectable antiquity are not to be lightly cast aside; but nevertheless they must always be used with extreme caution.

These old writers never made any distinction between the biography and the panegyric. They would have considered themselves unfaithful to their duty if they doubted any story that seemed to them to be creditable to the subject of their work. Even if the story were palpably untrue, they would have no hesitation in admitting it if they imagined that it would do good to the reader. Often, too, they were led into anachronisms by asking themselves what *ought* the subject of their memoir to have done, and then answering that question according to the ideas of the age in which they themselves lived.

In making use of these ancient sources of information, there are therefore two errors which are to be avoided. In the first place, that credulity which accepts every story, no matter how far-fetched or improbable; and in the second place, that scepticism which refuses to acknowledge any groundwork of truth, because some of the accessories of the story are manifestly untrue.

The biographers fill up this period of Saint Patrick's life with varied and extensive travels. He visits Saint Martin at Tours, and remains with him four years. He also becomes for a time the disciple of Saint Germanus, and with him visits Britain and aids in refuting the Pelagian heresy. He crosses the Alps into Italy. He visits some islands in the Mediterranean, and in one of them obtains the miraculous crozier known as the 'Staff of Jesus,' which was venerated as a most precious relic up to the time of the Reformation. Finally, he repairs to Rome, is consecrated by Pope Celestine, and with the apostolic commission thus obtained, sets out for his work in Ireland.

We can trace to some extent the growth of the legend. In Patrick's own works we have no intimation that he ever came in contact with any of the eminent men of other lands, but he intimates that he had some connection with Gaul, his biographers therefore considered it only fitting that he should have been instructed by the great religious leaders of the age in that country. Accordingly the story of his having been the disciple of Martin and Germanus is the first to make its appearance. At a later time the Papal sanction was regarded as indispensably necessary, and consequently we find that the story of his consecration by Pope Celestine then came forth, and was accepted by all succeeding biographers.

Happily it is not necessary for us now to enter at any length on the question as to how much of this should be received, and how much rejected. We know that the influence of Martin and Germanus was largely felt in Ireland. They were the leaders of the movement towards monasticism in Gaul, and from that movement Ireland to a great extent obtained its inspiration. But this influence can easily be accounted for without supposing that there was any personal contact between Patrick and the Gaulish leaders. This part of the story may therefore be regarded as doubtful, but not impossible.

On the other hand, the assertion that Patrick was consecrated by Pope Celestine labours under the most serious difficulties; for Roman influence was conspicuously absent from Ireland, and in the century after the arrival of Patrick the Roman teachers were met with bitter, and one might almost say unreasoning, hostility. Moreover, the legend did not take its rise until a Romanizing party had sprung up in the Church. We can therefore scarcely allow that Patrick ever had a commission from Rome. Patrick himself mentions no call except the inward call of the Spirit. He believed that God had chosen him for the work, and believing that, he made a full and unreserved dedication of himself to the service.

CHAPTER III.

MISSIONARY LABOURS OF SAINT PATRICK.

On the subject of Patrick's missionary labours, he gives us but little information himself. He excuses himself, saying, 'It would be a long task to enumerate one by one my labours, or even a part of them. Briefly I may say that the very loving God has often delivered me from slavery, and from twelve perils by which my very life was endangered, besides many snares, and that which I am not able to express in words.'

But if he does not tell us much about his labours, he is not at all reticent as to the results which followed. 'Truly I am debtor to God,' he says, 'who has bestowed such great grace upon me, that through me many people should be born again in God, and that ministers should everywhere be ordained for this people newly come to the faith, whom the Lord took from the ends of the earth.' He tells us that the number of his converts is to be counted by many thousands;—that 'those who never had any knowledge of God and worshipped only idols and abominations have lately become the people of the Lord, and are called the sons of God,' and that these 'sons of the Scots and daughters of princes' were ready to suffer reproaches and persecution for the sake of Christ. That all this should be accomplished within the life of one man, and principally as the result of his exertions, is a fact almost unexampled in the history of the Church.

This success must be attributed to a variety of causes: the earnestness and zeal and faith of Patrick himself, the methods he employed, and the state of preparedness in which he found the people. The extracts already given from his own writings show sufficiently how truly the spirit of the missionary breathed in him. The methods that he employed show him to have been as wise and judicious as he was pious.

We shall often have occasion to speak of the tribal system of the Irish. During Patrick's life it was in full force. Each chieftain was like the father of a family, and those who belonged to his clan looked to him for direction and leadership in everything. Recognising this fact, Patrick always endeavoured in the first place to gain if possible the favour of the petty kings and bring them to the obedience of the faith. In many cases he was successful, and the conversion of the tribe followed as a matter of course. But the converts thus made were not left in what must have been at best a mere nominal Christianity. As soon as permission was obtained from those in power, a Christian settlement was formed, a small church was erected—generally an unpretending structure made of wattles and clay—and some one was placed in charge who was consecrated to the office of the ministry, and who undertook the further instruction of those who had expressed their willingness to adhere to the new faith.

On his arrival in Ireland, Patrick's first care was to visit his old master, in order that he might pay in money for his own ransom, and that so no loss might be sustained by the slave's desertion. He also hoped to gain him as a convert, and thus bestow on him a richer kind of wealth. This charitable project was frustrated by the strange conduct of the master. He heard that Patrick was approaching, and he knew that his former slave's persuasive powers were such that he could convince him of anything that he wished. Lest therefore he should be converted by the instrumentality of him who had once been his bondsman, he gathered all his valuables together into a house, set fire to it, and himself perished in the flames.

Having thus ineffectually endeavoured to discharge what he considered to be his first duty, Patrick hastened to present himself at the court of King Leary, the monarch of all Ireland. This was an undertaking of the greatest risk, but it was one which if successful would open the way as nothing else could for the spread of the Gospel.

It may be well here to explain that there were at this time five kings in Ireland, each of whom ruled over one of the provinces, nearly conterminous with those into which Ireland is at present divided, except that a fifth province, Meath, now included in Leinster, was then a separate kingdom. One of these kings—generally the ruler of Meath—was styled *Ard-Righ*, or chief king; and to him the provincial kings were supposed to render the same loyalty as was in turn paid to them by the lesser chieftains who held sway in their several districts.

The story as told by the biographers is a striking one, though overloaded with those embellishments of miracle which they deemed essential to the proper dignity of a saint. They tell us that on Easter Eve in the year 433, Saint Patrick found himself on the

Hill of Slane, in the county Meath. Here, although the elevation is inconsiderable, a very extensive view of the surrounding country is obtained. Beneath flows the river Boyne—beyond is the great plain of Magh Breagh—and the horizon is bounded by gentle hills, on one of which, the Hill of Tara, there stood at that time the king's palace, the chief residences of the Druids, and some other buildings connected with the seat of government.

Among the Christian ceremonies of that age was the custom of having illuminations on Easter Eve, to symbolize the enlightening of those who on Easter Day were to be admitted by baptism into the Church, and also as setting forth the issuing of the Light of Life from the darkness of death. In accordance with this custom Patrick and his companions had lighted their Easter fire on the night in question. At the same time a druidical ceremony was taking place on Tara Hill. This consisted also in the kindling of a fire.

Among all the Celtic nations these fire festivals have held a prominent place. At certain seasons— notably on the first day of May (Beltaine) and on the first day of November (Samhain)—all the fires in the country were extinguished under pain of death. The 'needfire,' obtained by friction, was then solemnly ignited by the Druids, and from this sacred flame all the domestic hearths were kindled. The custom no doubt had its origin in the worship of fire, though it afterwards came to be regarded as magical rather than a religious act. While the spark was being procured certain incantations were repeated, and it was believed that the prosperity of the ensuing season was secured by the due performance of the rite, because it was in this way that the sorcery to which famine and disease were invariably attributed would be rendered powerless. But it was also believed that if by any mischance the ceremony was not rightly carried out—if the correct words of the incantation were not used, or, worst of all, if any of the old fire were allowed to remain unquenched, the spell was broken; the witches and magicians could work their evil will unchecked, and disasters of every kind would most certainly follow.

The different versions of this story which have been handed down to us are not quite consistent. All agree in saying that it happened at Eastertide; but some say that the pagan festival was the Feast of Tara, which we know to have been held in November; according to some it was the Feast of Beltaine, which comes nearer to the time required; others again say that it was the king's birthday. It seems, however, that no pagan festival of which we have any record was held at exactly the same time as the Christian Easter. This should not lead us to reject the story altogether; for besides the fact that it is probable in itself, it must be remembered that the Celtic Druids did not use the Julian Calendar, and that therefore it is impossible for us to say exactly when any of their feasts were held; and besides, it was not unusual, in times of calamity— particularly when pestilence appeared among the cattle, to have a special kindling of the 'needfire.' Indeed, this last explanation is suggested to us by the fact that Patrick is said not to have been aware that the festival was being held, which could scarcely have been the case if it had been one of the ordinary annual ceremonies.

The spread of education and enlightenment have happily made it difficult for us to understand the terror which must have seized the assembly at Tara on that eventful night when in the midst of their solemnities, and while the Druids were still repeating their incantations, a light was discerned shining in the distance—the Easter flame kindled by Saint Patrick. No conclusion seemed possible but that this was the work of a magician, and one too who would cast his evil spell over the land and bring to them desolation and death. The priests on being consulted gave it as their opinion that if the fire were not quenched before morning it would fill the whole land, and they therefore urged the monarch to execute immediate vengeance on him who had transgressed the laws of their religion.

Accordingly, King Leary ordered horses and chariots to be got ready, and set off with a considerable retinue in the middle of the night, towards the Hill of Slane, at the foot of which he arrived after two or three hours' travelling. There he paused, having been advised not to trust himself within the circle of the magic fire, lest he should be bewitched by the mysterious stranger. A messenger was then sent, summoning Patrick to appear before the king. The Christian teacher gladly embraced the opportunity, hastened to present himself to the monarch, and when he perceived the armed retinue that came against him, he commenced chanting with his companions the appropriate words, 'Some put their trust in chariots, and some in horses; but we will walk in the name of the Lord our God.'

If he had at this moment shown the least timidity, nothing would have saved him; but the fearless manner in which he approached, though unarmed, together with the strange chanting, must have confirmed the idea in the minds of the pagans that they were in presence of a great magician. Patrick followed up his advantage vigorously, and offered to appear before the court at Tara. We can well believe that the king and his retinue would have been much better pleased if he had remained away, but they were afraid to refuse his offer, and accordingly within a few days he presented himself at the king's palace, ready to preach the Gospel and confute the Druids.

Amid all the extravagances and impossible miracles with which the story of his preaching at Tara has been embellished, it is easy to recognise the general drift of the arguments used on that occasion. Patrick did not deny the power of the Druids. He would have been entirely too far in advance of his age if he had not believed that all ministers of the false religions were more or less in league with the devil, and were able with his assistance to work many wonders. But though he admitted the power of the Druids, he contended that their power was limited, and that the great God, whose religion he proclaimed, was able to protect those who trusted in Him ' from every hostile savage power, the incantations of false prophets, the black laws of heathenism, the spells of witches and smiths and Druids, the knowledge that blinds the soul.'

He also seems to have urged that the Druids could use their powers only for destruction and evil, whereas the power of God was a manifestation of goodness. The heathen priests could bring calamities of different kinds—they could turn summer into winter and light into darkness; but they were unable to reverse the process. Even the evils which they were able to inflict they were powerless to remove. But the almightiness of God was not only infinitely beyond any power wielded by the Druids —it was different in kind. It brought light and healing and blessing instead of cursing and destruction.

It will easily be understood that reasoning of this kind could scarcely fail to convince. The preacher stood before his audience as a living proof of the doctrine that he preached. The Druids professed to be able to destroy with their curse any one that opposed them. They were never weary of citing the case of Cormac Mac Art, the greatest of the ante-Christian kings, who, they said, was choked by a fish-bone because he had denied the truth of their idolatrous religion. But Patrick publicly defied them, and showed in himself that they were utterly powerless.

On more than one occasion they tried to destroy him by stealth. On his way to Tara they laid wait for him, but he managed to elude the ambush, and when the would-be assassins reported that nothing passed them except eight deer followed by a fawn, the astonished people jumped to the conclusion that this herd of deer was nothing else than the saint and his companions miraculously disguised.

All this explains to some extent the fact that Patrick was listened to from the first, and that his success was assured from the moment he stood before the king. But there was another and still more powerful reason which must not be kept out of sight. It is this; that Patrick was a man of faith, that he had the love of God in his heart, and an earnest desire to bring men to the knowledge of the truth, and that the truth which he preached was the simple Gospel of the grace of God.

As an example of the doctrines that he preached, and as showing to some extent the spirit in which he undertook his work, we may here quote the hymn commonly known as *Saint Patrick's Breastplate*. The original is written in Irish of a very ancient dialect, and it is quoted in the seventh century as the work of Saint Patrick. As it partakes somewhat of the nature of a Creed, it will tell us some of the beliefs of the ancient Irish Church.

SAINT PATRICK'S BREASTPLATE.[1]

I bind to myself to-day,
The strong power of an invocation of the Trinity,
The faith of the Trinity in Unity,
The Creator of the Elements.

I bind to myself to-day,
The power of the Incarnation of Christ, with that of His Baptism,
The power of the Crucifixion, with that of His Burial,
The power of the Resurrection, with the Ascension,
The power of the coming to the Sentence of Judgment.

I bind to myself to-day,
The power of the love of Seraphim,
In the obedience of Angels,
In the hope of Resurrection unto reward.
In the prayers of the noble Fathers,
In the predictions of the Prophets,
In the preaching of Apostles,
In the faith of Confessors,
In the purity of Holy Virgins,
In the acts of Righteous Men.

I bind to myself to-day,
The power of Heaven,
The light of the Sun,
The whiteness of Snow,
The force of Fire,
The flashing of Lightning,
The velocity of Wind,
The depth of the Sea,
The stability of the Earth,
The hardness of Rocks.

I bind to myself to-day,
The Power of God to guide me,

---

[1] From Todd's *Life of St. Patrick*, p. 246.

The Might of God to uphold me,
The Wisdom of God to teach me,
The Eye of God to watch over me,
The Ear of God to hear me,
The Word of God to give me speech,
The Hand of God to protect me,
The Way of God to prevent me,
The Shield of God to shelter me,
The Host of God to defend me,
   Against the snares of demons,
   Against the temptations of vices,
   Against the lusts of nature,
   Against every man who meditates injury to me,
     Whether far or near,
     With few or with many.

I have set around me all these powers,
   Against every hostile savage power,
   Directed against my body and my soul,
   Against the incantations of false prophets,
   Against the black laws of heathenism,
   Against the false laws of heresy,
   Against the deceits of idolatry,
   Against the spells of women and smiths and Druids,
   Against all knowledge which blinds the soul of man.

Christ protect me to-day,
   Against poison, against burning,
   Against drowning, against wound,
   That I may receive abundant reward.

Christ with me, Christ before me,
   Christ behind me, Christ within me,
   Christ beneath me, Christ above me,
   Christ at my right, Christ at my left,
   Christ in the fort,
   Christ in the chariot-seat,
   Christ in the poop.

Christ in the heart of every man who thinks of me,
   Christ in the mouth of every man who speaks to me,
   Christ in every eye that sees me,
   Christ in every ear that hears me.

     I bind to myself to-day,
The strong power of an invocation of the Trinity,

The faith of the Trinity in Unity,
The Creator of the Elements.
> Salvation is of the Lord,
> Salvation is of the Lord,
> Salvation is of Christ,
May Thy salvation, O Lord, be with us evermore.

It is said that this hymn was composed by Patrick when he was about to appear before King Leary. In after times it was used as a kind of charm. It was believed that those who recited it were thereby protected from the assaults of demons, from poison, envy and from sudden death. Most of the old Irish hymns were put to a similar use at one time or another. 'Saint Columba's Breastplate,' for example, another composition of the early age, used to be recited by travellers as a protection on their journeys. There is nothing in the hymns themselves which would countenance the idea that they were originally composed with any such intent.

In Saint Patrick's Hymn it will be noticed that all those doctrines which a modern Evangelical Protestant would consider to be of the first importance are prominently asserted; the Trinity, the Incarnation of Christ, His Death and Resurrection, the need of God's help in all the varied circumstances of life, the intimate union of the soul with Christ, and the great fact that the Lord is the Author of our salvation.

On the other hand, the peculiarities of the Church of Rome are simply ignored. It has been urged that a mere omission proves nothing, and that Saint Patrick may have been as ready to invoke the Blessed Virgin and the saints as he was undoubtedly ready in every moment of difficulty to seek the help of the Lord Jesus Christ. But we have given characteristic extracts, the *Confession* of Saint Patrick, and from his *Letter to Coroticus*, and have quoted his hymn *in extenso*. These are the only extant works, and they speak for themselves. We have no contemporary evidence that he held any other beliefs. One thing is quite certain: the man who wrote such works as these was one who exalted Christ, and preached Christ, and realized the abiding presence of Christ, and knew well what was the great hope to place before perishing sinners.

Having dwelt at such length on Saint Patrick's preaching at Tara, it is not necessary that we should pursue his career any further. He went through the length and breadth of the land, but his method of procedure was always the same. He appealed in the first instance to the chiefs, and obtained from each one when possible a site on which to found a religious establishment. Here he left a small community, who continued the enterprise after he had gone; these in turn became centres of life and light; and thus the good work was carried on and strengthened. The accounts of his success may possibly be greatly exaggerated; but there can be little doubt that before his death there was scarcely a district in which the Gospel had not been preached, and few places where there were not some found who gave themselves up to the work of evangelization. Many—perhaps the great majority—may have been converts only in name; but even the mere outward profession brought them under the influence of Christian teaching; and doubtless it must have often happened that the man who had accepted baptism without much thought of its real import, was led afterwards to a true consecration of heart and mind to the Saviour.

CHAPTER IV.

CHARACTER OF THE ANCIENT IRISH CHURCH.

WE have now to ask, What were the distinguishing characteristics of the Church thus founded by Saint Patrick and his companions? Concerning the doctrinal teaching nothing need be added to what has been already said. We have seen that the great central truths of Christianity were clearly taught, and that as far as we can now judge, they were not obscured by those additions and corruptions which in after ages caused them to be almost forgotten. In some matters of organization and of rites and ceremonies the Church of Ireland stands by itself and is unique in the history of Christendom. Let us dwell for a short time on these peculiarities.

The first thing that strikes us in the state of the ancient Irish Church is its intensely monastic character. In other countries monasticism has formed one of the institutions of the Church. In Ireland the whole Church was monastic. Some writers have urged, as an explanation of this phenomenon, that there must have been an early connection between Ireland and the East—in fact, that Ireland owed its first knowledge of Christianity to an Eastern source.

Monasticism is undoubtedly of Eastern origin. It arose in times of persecution, when Christians, sooner than give up their faith, or even take outward part in the rites of heathenism, left the cities and took refuge in the deserts, sheltering themselves until the time of danger was over. All were not so enthusiastic. Many conformed outwardly to the pagan worship, and were allowed to remain in their homes unmolested. In this way the Christians were divided into two classes—those who preferred the desert to a denial of their faith, and those who, less inflexible in their principles, were ready to make concessions for the sake of peace. After the persecutions had ceased the two classes continued to be distinct. Men still retired to the desert, not now to escape from prison and torture and death, but from the worldly pleasures and pursuits that were absorbing the thoughts of men and hindering them from paying due attention to their eternal interests. Naturally, the hermit was still regarded as the better Christian, when compared with him who continued in the world, and took part daily in the business and pleasures of life.

Amid all its extravagance, we can discern in this development of monasticism a germ of sound principle. Multitudes of those who professed Christianity when the profession began to be a mark of honour rather than disgrace knew little and cared less for the faith which they embraced. The name of Christ was on their lips, but the spirit of paganism was in their hearts. There were, no doubt, other and better ways in which earnest men could have protested against the formality of the age than that of separating themselves from their fellows, but still, it *was* a protest, and we know that in some ways it had its influence in directing men's minds to the paramount claims of our holy religion.

The institution soon grew in popularity and

spread rapidly, not only in the East, where it took its rise, but also in the West, where the more practical and less emotional disposition of the people would have led us to suppose it would never have found favour. Amongst its advocates were some of the greatest men of the age. Basil and Athanasius, Augustine and Jerome, Ambrose and Martin, and many besides, vied with one another in extolling the virtues of what was called the 'religious' life, and in inducing men and women to follow its rule.

The movement was at its height when Christianity was first preached in Ireland. Saint Martin had already founded his famous establishments at Tours and Poictiers. Tradition says that Saint Patrick was for a time an inmate of one of these monasteries. He certainly was very much influenced by the example that they presented. Full of enthusiasm for the system, he went forth, and wherever he obtained a footing his first care was to found a religious community.

The appearance presented by these establishments was as different as can well be conceived from anything that we have at the present day. A wall built of earth or of loose stones formed an enclosure, and served as a means of defence against enemies, as well as of separation from the rest of the tribe. Within this *cashel* or wall were the churches—exceedingly small of size, and quite unsuitable for anything approaching what might be called 'stately' worship. Any one who has ever seen the ruin of an Irish church belonging to the period before the twelfth century will not need to be told that the ritual of that age must have been of the simplest character possible. In some places there would be only one such church within the enclosure. In other places there might be as many as seven. Seven was indeed a favourite number, and the remains of these groups of seven churches are still to be found in several places, while the memory of seven churches formerly existing is continued by tradition in many others. They were all simple rectangular buildings, without chancels. All around the churches were grouped the cells of the members of the community—small bee-hive shaped huts, each inhabited by one or two or three of the inmates. Beside these there was sometimes a general refectory, where the meals were partaken in common, also a hall for penitential exercises, and possibly some other buildings. There would also be a cemetery—occasionally two, one for the women and another for the men. The churches were in like manner sometimes restricted to one sex. The buildings were mostly of wood, or of wattles daubed with clay; only rarely were they made of stone.

The remains of monasteries similar in many respects to the description just given have been found in the East. Like the Irish, they have the encircling wall, and the dwellings also are separate huts, instead of being one large building, as in the more modern establishments. The explanation of this resemblance is simple, and does not imply such immediate intercourse between Ireland and the East as has been supposed. All monastic establishments were originally much on the same model, but in the beginning of the sixth century a reformation of the system was brought about by Benedict, whose rule entirely superseded the older system in every country of Europe, Ireland excepted. In Ireland and the East alike his reforms were never received, and therefore the resemblances which we find arise from the survival in both places of the older form, when everywhere else it had become a thing of the past.

Another point must be kept in mind: that although there are remarkable resemblances between Eastern and Irish monasteries—resemblances sufficient to make it probable that they were both derived from the one original—yet the differences between them are still more remarkable. Let us briefly trace some of these differences.

Before the introduction of Christianity, the Druids formed communities similar in many respects to the early monasteries. They were not only priests, but lawgivers, philosophers, historians, teachers and bards. To all these offices the Christian ecclesiastics succeeded. Their establishments were not only centres of religious worship, but schools where whatever learning the land possessed could alone be found. In them, too, the laws of the land were made, for neither in pagan nor Christian times were the kings lawgivers merely by virtue of their office. In some cases a monarch of exceptional wisdom was also an *ollav*, but as a general rule the duty devolved on the wise men who by natural ability and a long course of mental training had been prepared for the office.

It is needless to say that such 'wise men' were found not among the warriors, but among the religious communities. This will perhaps explain the curious phenomenon that the ancient laws of Ireland had no 'sanction' beyond the force of public opinion. The *brehon* or judge was in reality a mere arbitrator, and had no way of enforcing his decisions. It is also a remarkable instance of the survival of old customs that we find at the present day the unwritten law of public opinion to be regarded by the native Irish as infinitely more sacred than the law of the land.

Englishmen cannot understand this, and it forms one of the great difficulties in the government of the country.

The bards were also for the most part taken from among the monks. The great Columba was himself a bard. These kept alive by their songs the memory of the heroes, and were in fact the historians of the land. All this so revolutionized monasticism that it became in Ireland an entirely different thing from what it had ever been in the Thebaid of Egypt. In every important feature it is easier to find contrasts than resemblances. The Irish monks, if monks they can be called, were not of a kind who separated themselves from the world and the interests of men. On the contrary, they became at once an important factor in society. They instructed the youths and legislated for the people in time of peace, and they advised and encouraged the heroes in time of war.

How far celibacy was practised or encouraged in these communities it is difficult for us now to say. Most of the information we possess comes from men who found it impossible to conceive the idea of a monastic life without the vow of celibacy. Yet even they have preserved enough to show that such a vow was far from being of universal acceptance. All authorities agree in telling us that Saint Patrick's father was a deacon, and his grandfather a priest, and he himself states the fact as if there was nothing in it unusual or that required explanation. Very many monasteries were open to both sexes—a state of things to which we shall again refer when we come to speak of the position of women in the ancient Irish Church.

A curious document exists which is supposed to have been composed in the middle of the eighth century.[1] In this we are told that there were three classes of Irish saints, the first of which was *most holy*, the second *very holy*, and the third *holy*. The first class was like the sun, the second like the moon, the third like the stars. The first order, the most holy, were led by Patrick, and had one Head, Christ. Of these, it is said that 'they rejected not the services and society of women, because, founded on the rock Christ, they feared not the blast of temptation.' The second order, however—very holy, although not as holy as the first, and later in date —' refused the services of women, separating them from the monasteries.' The kind of monastic life revealed in this description of the first order, and which is said to have existed for a considerable time, shows how much the ideal of the East had been modified before it found favour in the eyes of the western islanders.

When we come to the legends of the saints we meet with evidence at every step that both sexes were to be found together in the monasteries. Not that these legends are at all to be taken as serious history. It would require a very large share indeed of faith to receive the half of what they tell us. But we may be certain that they never contain anything that would be considered improper or unworthy of a saint, according to the ideas of the age in which they were composed; and if they record that women were commonly found in the monasteries, it may be taken as a plain proof that it was then neither an unusual nor unheard-of occurrence. To this may be added the fact that until a very late

---

[1] See this document given in full in Haddan and Stubbs' *Councils and Ecclesiastical Documents relating to Great Britain and Ireland*, vol. ii., p. 292. Dr. Todd gives a translation in his *Life of St. Patrick*, p. 88, note.

period there is abundant evidence that in some cases at least the highest ecclesiastics were married men.

The monastic system was still further modified by the spirit of clanship which pervaded all Irish institutions of that age. The Irish chiefs were nominally subject to the kings, but within their own territory they were absolute masters, and wielded a power of life and death over their subjects. It is said that these powers were sometimes shamefully abused, but if so, the abuse did not prevent the members of the tribe from rendering the most faithful adherence and obedience to the hereditary chief. The same spirit was imported into the religious communities. As Montalembert well says, 'The great monasteries of Ireland were nothing else, to speak simply, than clans reorganized under a religious form. From this cause resulted the extraordinary number of their inhabitants, which were counted by hundreds and thousands, and from this also came their influence and productiveness, which were still more wonderful.' In some cases, the original grant of a site carried with it the right of chieftainship, and the ecclesiastical superior thus became the head of the tribe. In others the lay element prevailed, and the chief who led the warriors to battle presided also over the affairs of the monastery. Generally, however, the rule was that the monastic superior should be chosen from the ruling family, and in all cases the monastery and the clan were so closely connected that the interest of the one was identical with the interest of the other.

The clanship of the Irish had its influence on the Church another way. As each tribe was practically independent of all others, and settled its own affairs in its own way, it was natural that each tribe would desire to have its own bishop. It would never have been tolerated by the chiefs nor desired by the subjects that one belonging to another clan should in any way have authority beyond the circle of his own people. Accordingly we find at a very early age the number of bishops was increased abnormally. Every tribe — in some cases every family—had its own bishop. The present 'rural deaneries' were nearly all ancient bishoprics, and they correspond almost invariably with the territories of the old Irish tribes.

Moreover, as the abbot was a kind of chieftain, and generally near of kin to the ruling house, it is plain that the principle of selection in his case was different from that which would regulate the choice of bishops, and that it would often happen that the abbot would be both unsuitable and unwilling to hold the episcopal office. Under such circumstances, the spirit of clanship led the people to cling to their leader, that is, the abbot, and put the bishop in the second place. The result was that the office of bishop was entirely dissociated from territorial authority—he had no diocese—and the cases were numerous where he was under the control of the abbot, exercising episcopal functions only under his direction. This, in its turn, led to a further increase in the number of bishops. As none of them had a see in the modern sense of the word, and therefore there was no possibility of one prelate interfering with the jurisdiction of another, it began to be a matter of pride in some monasteries to have a number of bishops amongst their inmates. In some cases it seems to have been the usage to have seven belonging to the same establishment. In the *Litany of Ængus the Culdee*, said to have been composed in the ninth century, there is a list of one hundred and forty-one places in Ireland where this institution of seven bishops existed. Saint Bernard informs us that up to the eleventh century there were no dioceses, bishops were multiplied and changed without order and regularity, so that almost every church had a bishop of its own.

A curious relic of the ancient system of clanship survives in the Irish Church to the present day. In most countries the churches and parishes are dedicated to a 'patron saint.' In Ireland the church was always called after the founder. It is at present easy to tell by the name whether a church has been founded before or after the Anglo-Norman invasion. If it be a church of Patrick, Columba, Kevin, or any Irish saint, it is almost certainly pre-Norman, and it is so called because the saint named founded, or is supposed to have founded, a church on the spot. But if it bear the name of St. Mary or St. Peter, or any saint not associated with Ireland itself, there need be no hesitation in deciding that its origin is to be looked for in that period when the combined influence of Rome and England was changing the old institutions. The reason is that in the ancient Irish Church every community was called the 'family' of the saint by whom it was first established, and each succeeding abbot was regarded as the successor of the founder, inheriting in the church a chieftainship which was similar in many ways to the chieftainship which the leader of the tribe inherited.

There is an old poem extant which purports to give a list of those who composed the 'family' of Saint Patrick. It is found in one of the ancient biographies of Patrick, and has also been copied into the *Annals of the Four Masters*. If it is in any way a fair description of what an ecclesiastical family was in the early ages, it presents us with a picture very different from anything that we have been accustomed to associate with the monastic life. Instead of speaking of a monastery, we would be more inclined to call it an industrial colony—a tribe of men and women who in the midst of a warlike nation devoted themselves entirely to the arts of peace.

Several bishops and priests are mentioned as members of this family; but from amongst them, one bishop, named Sechnall, and one priest, named Moehta, are singled out as those who use their office for the special benefit of the community. The others, although ecclesiastics in rank, occupy themselves in secular duties. Bishop Erc, for example, acts as judge, and Bishop Maccaeirthinn has the still more secular office of champion, or mighty man. From this we may conclude that the community was free from outside control, that it made its own laws, and carried on its own wars. The presence of a champion and a body of armed retainers was most necessary, for the rival kings and chiefs often attacked the monasteries. We have also reason to believe that in some (let us hope exceptional) cases the religious communities themselves carried on aggressive warfare, and attacked one another with a vigour which their secular neighbours could not surpass.

Of those who are mentioned as priests we have Mescan the brewer, Bescna the poet, Manach the woodman, and Logha the helmsman. Other officers were the singer, the chamberlain, the bell-ringer, the true cook (the expressive adjective shows how his services were appreciated), three smiths, three artificers, a charioteer, a shepherd, and a scribe. Nor were the women forgotten. The two daughters of Gleaghrann, famous for their beauty, were members of the family, and three other ladies are named, including Lupait, Patrick's own sister, who exercised daily their skill in embroidery. That men and women enjoyed unrestricted social intercourse is shown by the fact that scandals sometimes arose. Of the three embroideresses, two were at one time more or less under a cloud. It was deemed advisable that Lupait should not continue any longer under the same roof as her nephew Mel, although he was a 'saint' and a bishop; and another lady, Erc, was only cured of her passion for Benin the singer by an illness which brought her to death's door.

Once more, it is well to remark that these accounts are not to be taken as history. It never happened that all those mentioned as belonging to the family of Saint Patrick formed members of the same establishment. What we do learn is, that at a much later period than the time of Patrick the ideal of an ecclesiastical community was an association where both sexes met on equal terms; where the services of the Church were duly celebrated; where copies of the Scriptures and of other books were made; where workers in metal and wood and stone pursued their avocations; where the different operations of husbandry were carried on; where the brethren were averse to war, yet able and ready to defend themselves when called on; where excursions by land and water, in the chariot and in the boat, were not infrequent. All this must be borne in mind when we speak of the monastic character of the Irish Church. It bears out fully the view expressed above, that these families would be better described as industrial colonies or Christian communes than by the more usual but misleading name of monasteries.

It will be seen that the constitution of the Irish Church was one that suited itself to the character of the people. This conformity to their national institutions must have aided considerably in the rapid spread of the Gospel amongst them. Nevertheless, it was not altogether an advantage. Under the Druidical system the duties of religion were for the most part vicariously performed. The priests offered the sacrifices, pronounced the incantations, and performed the rites that were necessary, and the fighting men rested content that the favour of heaven had been secured, although they themselves took no part in the religious exercises, and never dreamt of their religion having any effect on their lives. It is to be feared that a state of things almost similar existed when the tribe nominally had become Christian. The warriors were bloodthirsty and cruel as of old, and left the duties of religion to be performed by those who had given themselves up to that particular work. At one time, Ireland was known as the Island of Saints. The history of the country in that age is somewhat disappointing, and would lead us to doubt whether the flattering title was deserved. It differs but little from the history of other periods. We have the same war and bloodshed, the same turbulence and disunion. The explanation is simply this: that two nations, as it were, existed—the one given up to the offices of religion, to the production of books and the pursuit of learning—the other retaining all the lawless and turbulent spirit which had characterized the land from of old. There are few countries in the world where such incongruous elements can exist side by side. But even at the present day it is to some extent the same. Men have been known to pause in the excitement and frenzy of a faction fight and respectfully wait while a funeral passes by, only to break out the moment after in the same untamed and untameable fury.

The other distinguishing characteristics of the Irish Church are its missions and its independence of the see of Rome. The former will occupy our attention when we come to consider the work of Saint Columba and his companions, and of others who left Irish shores to found communities in different countries. The latter will be dealt with in connection with the controversies to which it gave rise.

CHAPTER V.

SAINT COLUMBA.

In the last chapter we have been considering institutions rather than events. But in truth the events of the period can for the most part be only vaguely guessed. We know more of the results than of the processes by which they were brought about. We can plainly see that a great transformation was effected in Ireland—that whereas the first years of the fifth century saw her entirely pagan, the early years of the sixth century saw her entirely Christian.

In the meantime, events of the highest importance were happening both in Britain and on the continent of Europe. It was in this century that the great empire of Rome came finally to an end. The last of the Cæsars was dethroned, and a barbarian usurper ruled over the mistress of the world. It was in this century too that Gaul became France, and Britain became England. The only influence that these revolutions had upon Ireland was of a negative character, although it was none the less important on that account. They cut off Ireland, to a great extent, from European influences. The wars in France and Italy—the overthrow of kingdoms and setting up of new dynasties—finally, the conversion to Christianity of the barbarian conquerors: these were events that so occupied the minds of men that there was no time to think of the lone island in the Western Sea, which all the time was undergoing a revolution, more peaceful, but none the less important, and was founding and developing its Christian institutions in its own way—modifying them and adapting them, as we have seen, by its own native genius.

The invasion and subjugation of England made this isolation more complete. The Angles and other German tribes who landed in England, unlike their brethren on the Continent, were bitterly hostile to the faith of the people whose lands they seized. The Gauls submitted to and made friends with their conquerors, and the result was that they soon brought them under the power of their religion and civilization. The Britons, on the contrary, contested every inch of their territory, and provoked a war of extermination, in which their nation and religion were alike obliterated. The testimony of language witnesses to us what a radical difference there was in the two cases. When the Franks conquered Gaul, its language was Latin; but that language of the vanquished held its ground, and quite overcame the tongue of the victors, so that modern French may be said to be the direct lineal descendant of the language spoken before the conquest. The English tongue, on the other hand, has not been appreciably influenced by the ancient British. The Celtic element is insignificant at the best, and has been in great part derived from other sources. Thus it happened that while Ireland was being converted to Christianity, a reverse process was taking place in England. There the old British Church was being destroyed, and heathenism was being set up in its place. The effect of this was to introduce a bitterly hostile and unbelieving nation which, like a wedge, separated the Christian Church of Ireland from the Christian countries of Europe.

In the north of Britain the Picts continued still practising the rites of Druidism. They were the only tribe of Celts which had remained unevangelized. They were on more or less friendly terms with the Scots or Irish—making common cause with them occasionally against the British. It seemed natural therefore that the establishment of Christianity, which had begun so auspiciously and progressed so favourably in Ireland, should also be accomplished among those tribes who were of the same race, followed the same manner of life, and had the same tribal organization. The story of how the Irish Church undertook this work and carried it to a successful issue is one of the most interesting, as it is one of the best authenticated in her whole history, and deserves to be told at some length.

In the year 521, that is, about ninety years after the coming of Saint Patrick, Columba was born. He was of the family of the O'Donnells, and was nearly related to the royal house which held sway in the north of Ireland and south-west of Scotland. The story of his early life was written after his later years had shed much lustre on his name, and we are not therefore astonished to find that it is filled with many presages of his future greatness. When quite a youth he became a disciple at one of the large monastic schools for which Ireland was soon to become famous, and at the early age of twenty-five he is said to have himself founded a school and religious establishment at the Oak Grove of Calcaigh, which was the ancient name of Londonderry. Similar establishments were founded at Durrow in the King's County, Kells in Meath, Moone in Kildare, Swords near Dublin, and other places. His after life shows him to have been a man of great determination, strong will and considerable ability. It is therefore not at all improbable that the legend here preserves the truth, and that these and possibly many other foundations owe their origin to his early zeal. We should have heard little about him, however, if it were not for what many would call a strange chance, but which was in reality a remarkable dispensation of Providence, which changed the whole course of his life.

Columba was visiting at the monastery of Saint Finnen of Moville, and while there obtained the loan of a copy of the Psalter. The translation must have been different from that to which he had been accustomed, for he desired at once to obtain one like it for himself. Finnen, however, seemed to think that the value of his book would be diminished if it were not unique of its kind, and Columba knew that it would be useless to ask him to allow a copy to be made. So he secretly worked by night, when he thought that he was unobserved, and in a short time had made for himself the copy that he desired. Unfortunately, the secret was not as well kept as he had imagined. Finnen was made aware of what was being done, and in the end made a claim, that as the original was his, the copy belonged to him also. Columba very naturally failed to see the matter in that light. He had with his own hand made the copy, and he point blank refused to part with it. Ultimately the matter was brought before King Dermaid, who gave the remarkable judgment, 'To every cow belongs its calf, therefore to every book belongs its copy.' This only roused the temper of Columba, who, still holding to his precious possession, replied, 'This in an unjust decision, O Dermaid, and I will avenge it on you.' Other causes of irritation followed. An open rupture ensued, and Columba escaped from Tara, fled to the north of Ireland, roused the clans of the O'Donnells, and challenged the king to battle.

In all this, it is well to remark, we have a good example of the system of clanship already described, which pervaded the Church. Columba here acted in exactly the same way as one of the chieftains would have acted if he imagined himself to have been insulted. The result in this case was a battle fought at Cooldreeny, near Sligo, in which Columba and the O'Donnells were victorious, and the King of Ireland was forced to retreat, after three thousand Meath warriors had been laid dead on the field.

The king, worsted in battle, had recourse to other methods. The great fair of Teltown was one of the old institutions of the country. People flocked to it from all parts for the transaction of business, the celebration of games, and the holding of national assemblies. There the king called together a synod to consider the case. Teltown was in the heart of Meath, and we can therefore well understand that although men came from all quarters, the Meath men would be in an overwhelming majority. Accordingly, when Columba appeared before them he found himself in presence of a hostile assembly. In spite of the spirited support which he received from some—notably from Brendan, the Abbot of Birr—a sentence of excommunication was pronounced against him for having been the cause of so much bloodshed.

Columba himself, like many another man of hot temper, was soon sorry for what he had done. In the moment of irritation he had not thought that such terrible loss of life would result from his impetuosity. Nothing shows more clearly the depth and reality of his religious life than the way in which he acknowledged and openly confessed his fault. Nor was his repentance merely in word. He was resolved to exhibit in his life the penitence which he expressed with his lips, and with this end in view he repaired to his 'soul friend,' Molaise of Devenish, and consulted with him how he could make atonement for the evils which he had caused. The advice given was that he should leave Ireland, devote himself to missionary work amongst the heathen Picts, and labour until as many had been won for Christ as had been lost in the battle of Cooldreeny. With a heavy heart, but with firm determination, Columba at once accepted the task thus proposed to him, took with him twelve companions, as well as a retinue of followers, and sailed from the shores of his native country. They first landed on the Island of Oronsay, but as the hills of Ireland were still in view they took again to their boats, pursued their way farther to the north, and eventually settled on the Island of Iona.

In crossing the sea they were not parting from their own countrymen. The south-western portion of Scotland formed the territory of what was practically one of the tribes of Ireland. It was the only part of North Britain that bore the name Scotland; that is, the country of the Scots or Irish. Among the many changes that time has effected in the names of places, none is more remarkable than that the mother country, Ireland, whence all the Scots came, should no longer be called Scotland, and that Alba, as North Britain was then called, should appropriate to itself the name of what was at first one of the smallest provinces. The ruler of this Irish kingdom in Scotland, or, as it would be more correctly expressed, Scotic kingdom in Alba, was a near kinsman to Columba, and therefore the right to settle in the island was secured without any difficulty; the favour and protection of the prince were given as a matter of course, and the members of the community set about building a monastic village, formed exactly after the pattern of those to which they had been accustomed in Ireland.

The story of Patrick's preaching was now, as it were, repeated. Pursuing the same tactics, Columba presented himself first of all before Brude, King of the Picts. His success was great from the very beginning. Notwithstanding some opposition, he obtained the protection of the prince, and had permission to go through the land for the purpose of preaching. His biographers tell us of his many miracles, by which he silenced the adversaries and won the respect of the people; Bede, with more truth, tells us that 'he converted the nation to the faith of Christ by his preaching and example.' From that time, and for some centuries following, the little island of Iona became a centre of religious life. Isolated from the rest of the world, it was uninfluenced by the great movements which were causing changes in other countries. Even such matters as the reform of the calendar were unknown in the little northern island, where the community continued their round of fast and festival, unconscious of the fact that their times differed from all the rest of Christendom.

In other and more important things the difference was still more clearly marked. The monastic reforms of Benedict were working great changes among the religious communities of the West; but their influence was bounded by the sea. Even in South Britain they were long unknown—while in Ireland

and Iona centuries elapsed before they were introduced. The general tendency of the Church in that age was towards increased splendour of ceremonial, but in Iona the same simple unpretending worship continued as heretofore. Their sanctuary was still only a lowly thatched building made of clay, and much of their worship must have been conducted in the open air. The cultus of the Virgin Mary and the practice of the Invocation of Saints were spreading rapidly throughout Christendom; but Iona knew nothing of them. The universal supremacy of the see of Rome was beginning to be a recognised doctrine. Innocent and Leo had both reigned before Iona was established; Gregory had become Pope while Columba himself was still living; but these great names were almost unknown at Iona. There was little communication between distant countries in that early time; and especially when a land was far removed from the highways of commerce, it knew little indeed of what was going on in the world around, and was simply beyond the influence of the thoughts and opinions that were moving men's minds in other countries. Hence it is that we have in Ireland and in Iona a survival for several centuries of Church life as it existed elsewhere in the beginning of the fifth century.

The earliest Life of Saint Columba was written by Adamnan, who was born about twenty-five years after Columba's death, and who became afterwards his successor as Abbot of Iona. He was thus removed by only one generation from the subject of his biography, and he must have known and conversed with many who had seen the saint. His work is interesting in many ways—not the least as showing how short a time it requires for a name to become surrounded with a whole atmosphere of myth and legend. The book is not a biography in the strict sense. The author does not pretend to give us a detailed account of the incidents of Saint Columba's life, but dwells first on the prophecies, secondly on the miracles, and thirdly on the visions of the saint. As may well be supposed, many of the anecdotes he relates must have been simple ordinary events, which may easily have happened without any miraculous element at all. But Adamnan sees miracles in everything. He revels in the extraordinary; and as we read story after story, in some places one more impossible than the other, we are sorely tempted to give it all up in disgust. But notwithstanding all its improbable miracles, the book is most valuable. It was written while the isolation of Irish Church life was still to a great extent unbroken, and the incidental references it contains portray for us all the more truthfully, because unintentionally, the life led by the community at Iona in its earliest times; and as Iona was formed on the same pattern as the monasteries of Ireland, the description of it will enable us to picture to ourselves the kind of scene which they also presented.

We have to imagine to ourselves a centre of busy activity and cheerful toil. Members of the community were continually coming and going. Sometimes it would be on a missionary expedition to preach amongst the pagan Picts. At other times it would be to visit a king or chief with whom it was of importance to make a kind of treaty, or who was perhaps to be rebuked for some unlawful act that he had done. Often they went to treat for the ransom of captives, or to beg for pity on behalf of the conquered. Occasionally, too, they were sent to Ireland, where perhaps a synod was being held, or where it was necessary to visit their brethren, followers of the same rule in the different establishments, and bring advice from headquarters. Then when they returned, all the brethren would assemble, a report would be given of the results of their mission, and action would be taken accordingly.

Visitors to the settlement were not infrequent. Standing on the opposite shore, they shouted, as a signal that they desired to get across. Then some of the brothers embarked in their coracle,[1] and ferried them over the narrow strait. On arrival they were hospitably welcomed, and found a special house, the 'strangers' hospice' or 'guest room,' set apart for their entertainment.

These visitors were of a varied class. Perhaps it would be a slave who had fled from his master. This the brethren never encouraged; and while they protected the runaway, they endeavoured to persuade him to return to his service; though in some cases they begged for his freedom, or themselves provided the ransom that was necessary. Until the slave was thus made legally free, they would not receive him as a member of the community. Then, again, there were fugitives escaping from the avenger. Some of these were criminals; others were unjustly accused; but to all the monastery was a City of Refuge. When once within its shelter, they were sure they would not be slain without a fair trial, and that the judge would be one that would incline to mercy rather than to severity. Others came seeking medical advice, for the brethren were skilled in the virtues of herbs, and had cures for many ailments. Then there would be those who were pursued by the robber bands of hostile tribes. In the monasteries on the mainland

[1] The coracle is a small boat made of wicker work covered with skins.

the people would often come, carrying their valuables and driving their flocks and herds before them, for within the consecrated *Termon*[1] was the only place of safety. The transporting of cattle to Iona would not be an easy task, but the less cumbersome possessions would often be borne by fugitives across the waters. Some too would come to take counsel in their difficulties, spiritual and temporal; young men, in the enthusiasm of their early days, desiring to give up their lives to the work of the Lord; or perhaps old men, tormented by conscience, wanting to know how they could make atonement for a life of sin; sometimes even kings, desiring to explain the grounds of a quarrel before they would make a declaration of war. Then there would be brethren from other parts of the country; abbots and bishops, attracted by the renown of the saint, who would come to sit at his feet for a while—perchance to purchase from him one of his beautiful manuscripts, or to consult with him in some difficulty which had arisen in the administration of their office.

If the visitor were an eminent man, a special feast was made in his honour, and the laws of hospitality being considered paramount to those of ascetism, if he happened to come on a fast day (and they ordinarily fasted both Wednesday and Friday), the abstinence was foregone for that occasion, and the feast of welcome took its place. This was the custom in all the monasteries; for not only do we read of such feasts being given to distinguished strangers in Iona, but we find that the same compliment was paid to Columba when he went to visit other places, and we learn further that all the people in the neighbourhood were accustomed to contribute

---

[1] The *Termon* was the boundary of the monastic grounds. It was generally marked by a stone cross.

towards the banquet. As soon as the visitor arrived, one of the brothers proceeded to wash his feet, as a token that while he stayed with them they were all willing to wait upon him as his servants; because, too, the Irish Church at that time retained many Jewish ordinances, among which was the frequent washing of feet before entering upon the services of the sanctuary. At the ninth hour they partook of the common meal. The bread was blessed according to the example of our Lord, and then the company of the brethren partook of it, the strangers at the same time joining the party. But though there was thus a hearty welcome, the visitor was not allowed to prolong his stay indefinitely. If he meant to remain for any great length of time, he was required to take his place in the community, which of course meant that he would have to do his part in the regular work of the establishment.

This work was of a varied character. Some of the inmates were 'hardy fishermen,' who plied their task in the not very peaceful waters that surrounded them. Probably these also looked after the seals, which were 'preserved' by the islanders, and seem to have been used by them as an article of food. Other members of the community tilled the ground, and as the day wore on, the prior drove round in his chariot and visited them at their work. At Iona they all worked in common, and made their way home to their abodes in the evening, often very wearied, particularly in harvest time, and each one carrying a heavy load. It was a kind of family life that they lived, and we are told how Columba used to be always grieved when they returned late to the monastery. In other places — Clonmacnois, for example—each of the brethren seems to have had his own piece of land to till, for which he was held responsible. Besides the tilling of the ground there was the work of tending the animals. Night and morning the milk had to be carried from the 'milking field,' and as each returned thus laden, he paused at the door of Columba's cell, and obtained the saint's blessing. A horse was also employed in this daily task of carrying the milk. Then there was occasional building work to be done. Some of the huts were made of wooden planks, and the timber had to be hewn and prepared for them. This was at times very hard work, especially when storm and rain had to be encountered. Other huts were formed of wattles and clay. Although these did not require the same expenditure of labour at first, they must have been very often in need of repair. Boats, too, had to be built; frail crafts they were, made of wicker covered with skin, yet wonderfully long voyages were sometimes taken in them. Then there was the work of the household. The butcher, the cook and the baker are mentioned, showing that there was a division of labour, in which each had his own task.

The most important business of all, and that for which the Columban monasteries were famous, was the writing and illuminating of copies of the Scriptures. At Iona this work was carried on continuously, and was under the special superintendence of Columba himself. He made it a rule that none of his establishments should be without a copy of the Word of God, and most of the books which were thus scattered through the length and breadth of the land were produced at Iona. The magnificent copy of the Gospels known as the Book of Kells, now in the library of Trinity College, Dublin, though not, as had once been imagined, as old as the time of Columba, is scarcely a century later in date, and was most undoubtedly produced by the brethren who followed his rule. It is by far the most beautifully illuminated manuscript of its age in existence. The greatest care was taken that these copies should be correct. After the writing was finished a number of brethren carefully examined it, lest there should be any error or omission. Then it was jealously preserved in a cover made of precious metal, and a leathern satchel was used to protect it from any injury. It is said that on the day before Columba's death, although his increasing bodily weakness made him conscious that his end was approaching, he was still at his favourite work, and sat for some time in his cell, transcribing the Psalter. At last he came to the words (Ps. xxxiv. 10), 'They that seek the Lord shall not want any good thing.' 'Here, he said, at the end of this page I must stop. Let Baithen write that which follows. The last verse that he wrote was indeed suitable to the saint who was then passing away, for to him eternal good things shall never be wanting. And the verse following was equally suitable to the father who succeeded him, the teacher of his spiritual children: "Come, ye children, hearken unto me; I will teach you the fear of the Lord." And he did succeed him, as Columba had advised, not in teaching alone, but in writing.'[1] We shall see afterwards that there is reason to believe that not only was the work of transcription thus carried on continually, but that the Irish, or at all events the Celtic Church, produced translations of the Scriptures for itself, differing in many important ways from the translations in use elsewhere.

Admission to the monastery was easily procured.

[1] Adamnan, *Vit. Columb.*, iii. 23.

No novitiate was required, and if vows were taken, they were not necessarily lifelong. Any member of the community could return to the world when he pleased. No one was admitted, however, who had a father or a mother dependent on him for support. Even when there were younger brothers able to perform the duty, the parents could not be deserted until a guarantee had been obtained that the younger would take the place of the elder. Married couples were not allowed to separate. The story is told of a woman who sought admission to the convent, and offered to do anything that the saint desired her, provided he did not ask her to live with her husband, whom she hated. The saint simply took the unhappy pair, fasted and prayed with them, and continued these religious exercises without intermission, until at last they agreed to be reconciled, when he sent them away, united in affection, to live happily all the rest of their lives.

As to the doctrines taught, little need be added to what has been already said. They taught in Scotland exactly the same truths which Saint Patrick had enforced in Ireland. The Venerable Bede tells us that the Bible was their one rule of faith, to the exclusion of all other. 'They had none,' he says, 'to bring them the synodal decrees for the observance of Easter, by reason of their being so far away from the rest of the world; wherefore they only practised such works of piety and chastity as they could learn from the prophetical, evangelical and apostolical writings.'[1] Men who were led by such a rule might of course make some mistakes—mistakes, the importance of which would perhaps be magnified by those who imagined themselves to be better instructed—

---

[1] Bede, *Eccl. Hist.*, iii. 4, Bohn's Ed.

they might be quite unable, for example, to calculate the right time for keeping Easter; they might continue to follow customs that were never intended to be permanent; they might exaggerate the importance of precepts that were intended to be only partial and local in their application : but in every essential point they must have been in the right way. Those who practise the works of piety and chastity which they learn from the prophetical, evangelical and apostolical writings cannot do so without receiving the inward light of the Holy Spirit, and being led to place their trust in Him of whom all these writings testify.

As Christianity was first preached in Ireland at the beginning of the fifth century, the impress of that age continued for long afterwards. The peculiar monasticism, which was such a striking feature of Irish Christianity, and which was reproduced at Iona, was an example of this. So were also the severe penances of which we sometimes read (though not in connection with Iona), the practice of praying for the dead, and the use of the sign of the cross. We may trace the germ—although only the germ—of auricular confession in the institution of 'soul friends,' which will be more fully explained farther on. They were advisers rather than confessors, but we can easily see how the one would readily develop into the other. As yet, however, confession was public; the penance imposed was also public, and absolution was not given until the required penance was complete.

More remarkable was the existence of some practices which we are accustomed to regard as Jewish. We have already alluded to the washing of feet before entering the sanctuary. They had also the distinction of meats into clean and unclean.

Vessels too became ceremonially unclean when any defiling substance had come in contact with them. This usage enabled them at one time to show their abhorrence of Romish teachers in a peculiarly irritating manner. Whenever a vessel had been used by one of those who followed the foreign rule, the Irish ostentatiously cleansed it, as if it had been defiled by the contact. They observed the Jewish ordinance of the Levirate marriage, that when a man died and left no seed, his brother should take his wife and raise up seed unto his brother. Consecrated salt was used in some ceremonies. Baptism was administered by preference in running water, and was most probably by immersion. This is mentioned in the lately-discovered *Teaching of the Twelve Apostles* as having been an early custom in other places. Some of these usages became modified afterwards; but there is abundant evidence that in the earlier times they were all observed.

A closer bond of union joined the several establishments where the rule of Saint Columba was followed than was usual in Ireland. True to the tribal instincts, the abbacy was confined to the kinship of the founder; but in the election of abbots all the Columban monasteries seem to have taken part, and the Abbot of Iona, who was in some measure the head of the order, might have been chosen from any of them. They regarded themselves as the same brotherhood, though living in different places and under different rulers; and this federation of the several monasteries continued until a very late date.

Several incidents might be cited in illustration of this. For example, when Iona was attacked by the Norsemen in the beginning of the ninth century, the relics and valuable possessions of the community were transported to Kells. Again, in the eleventh century, we have the Kells workmen making a metal book-shrine for the O'Donnells of Donegal, to whom they owed allegiance because Columba was an O'Donnell. At a much later date, early in the thirteenth century, the Columban monastery of Derry sent some of its inmates to Iona to repel the Bishop of Man, who wanted to assert his authority, and had erected some buildings there. This was of course a considerable time after the Anglo-Norman invasion of Ireland, and shows how long the confederation, and to some extent the independence of the Columban monasteries, continued.[1]

[1] See Stokes' *Ireland and the Anglo-Norman Church*, where a most interesting chapter deals with the continuance of the Celtic Church in Ireland in Anglo-Norman times.

CHAPTER VI.

SAINT COLUMBANUS.

A GREAT missionary enterprise, like that which resulted in the establishment of a monastery at Iona, and through it the conversion of the whole nation of the Picts, bespeaks a Church in which energy and zeal are no rare virtues. But missionary labour has also a wonderful reflex action. It is the product of holy energy and zeal, and in turn it produces the same. It is the Churches most interested in missions that are ever foremost in undertaking new missions, and it is these also that are most in earnest about their own home work. The Pictish mission was almost, if not entirely, in the hands of the followers of Saint Columba; but their example provoked to jealousy many of the other communities which were established in Ireland. We are not therefore surprised to find that the generation which saw Columba and his companions landing at Iona, was quickly followed by one when Irish missionaries went forth in many directions, and became famous as evangelizers and teachers.

It is a curious coincidence that the most remarkable of these missionaries was a namesake of the great apostle of Scotland. He is generally known now by the name Columbanus, to distinguish him from the founder of Iona, who is always called Columba or Columkill. But it need hardly be pointed out that the two names are really the same. Both mean 'Dove.' The termination *kill* means 'Church'; so that Columkill is 'Dove of the Church.' The addition is said to have been made in token of the great piety which Columba exhibited at an early age.

Columbanus, of whom we have now to speak, belonged to the monastic school of Saint Comgal at Bangor in the County Down. It is said that there were three thousand scholars in this establishment. This is scarcely credible, the less so as we know that the old biographers never stuck at a little exaggeration. On the other hand, if they exaggerate the numbers, they altogether underrate the learning with which these old schools abounded, for they were quite unable to appreciate it. When we read their works we are sorely tempted to think that the men whom they commemorate were as narrow-minded, as credulous, as superstitious, and as ignorant as they were themselves; and then when we find places described in general terms, and in very bad Latin, as centres of learning and wisdom, we are somewhat inclined to put the learning and wisdom along with the miracles in that region of myth where everything is quite too unsubstantial and visionary for the founding of any serious historical argument.

Happily, we have better evidence than the writings of the biographers. In this case, for example, some of the works of Columbanus have come down to us, and they tell us what could be learnt in the old Irish schools, because it is certain that whatever learning he possessed was obtained before he left the country. From these works we find that he wrote Latin, both prose and verse, in excellent style; that he knew Greek, which was more than the Pope of Rome could have said; and that he was not unacquainted with Hebrew. He interprets his own name in the three languages, and says, 'I am called in Hebrew, Jonah; in Greek, Peristera; and in Latin, Columba.'[1] He not only knew these languages, but shows an acquaintance with Latin and Greek literature; and altogether his writings give us an entirely different idea of the progress that learning had made from that which we should have at first imagined. This school of Bangor seems to have been very jealous of the school of Iona. On one occasion the jealousy brought on actual warfare. At other times, however, the rivalry was of a healthier kind.

Columbanus was born in the year 543. He was therefore twenty-two years younger than his namesake of Iona. Of his early life in Ireland we have but little knowledge, except that he studied at several schools before he became a disciple of Comgal at Bangor. It was not until after his fortieth year that he began his missionary labours. First, he passed over to England, and from thence he made his way to France. His idea had been to have gone farther, and to have spent his energies in the evangelization of the heathen tribes beyond; but he found that there was no necessity to seek farther than the nominal Christians of Gaul, who seem to have gained little more than a new superstition from their conversion, while they retained all the cruelty and treachery of barbarism.

At the invitation of Guntram, King of Burgundy, he settled in that country. He was absolutely fearless in his denunciations of sin, and like another

---

[1] Adamnan gives the same explanation in his *Life of Columba of Iona*.

John the Baptist stood before the highest in the land and rebuked them to their face. Like the Baptist, too, he attracted great multitudes to his preaching, and even the princes whom he reproved were contented to hear him gladly, and sometimes, like Herod, 'did many things,' though it is to be feared without any real change of heart. Still further bearing out the resemblance, it was through the interference of a wicked woman that his labours were in the end brought to an abrupt termination, though happily, in his case, they were not ended by martyrdom. Refusing to give his blessing to the illegitimate children of Theodoric II., which were presented to him by Brunehault, the queen regent, he excited her resentment, and this resentment followed him persistently, until she had prevailed on her grandson to banish the fearless monk from his dominions. He was placed on board a vessel, the intention being to send him to Ireland; but after it had put to sea a contrary wind drove them back again, and the master of the ship, taking this as a Divine intimation that Columbanus was not to go to Ireland, landed him at the mouth of the Loire, and went on his journey without him. From thence Columbanus made his way to Switzerland, where one of his followers, Saint Gall, was left behind, and founded the establishment which has given name to one of the cantons. Eventually, he settled in North Italy, where he founded the famous monastery of Bobbio, near which he died in the year 615.

The incidents in the life of Columbanus are full of interest, but are for the most part outside the scope of this present work. He was the great competitor with Benedict in the reformation of the monastic system; and such was his success and the popularity of his rule that at one time it seemed as if his influence, and not that of Benedict, was to change the aspect of monasticism in all succeeding ages. Moreover, his followers worked with such fearless and untiring activity, and presented in themselves such examples of self-denial and devotion, that, as has been well said, 'For a time it seemed as if the course of the world's history was to be changed; as if the older Celtic race that Roman and German had swept before them had turned to the moral conquest of their conquerors; as if Celtic and not Latin Christianity was to mould the destinies of the Churches of the West.'[1] All this, however, is beside our present purpose. We have only to consider the life and work of Columbanus in so far as it throws light on the history of the Church in Ireland, the country which sent him forth as an apostle and evangelist.

The rule which Columbanus imposed on those who were his followers is still extant, and is generally supposed to have been derived from that already in force in Comgal's establishment at Bangor. If so, Bangor must have been very different from Iona. The picture drawn in the last chapter of the life of those who looked up to Columba as 'father, is that of a peaceful Christian community, where the highest law is the law of love, and punishments, if they existed at all, occupy such a secondary place that they are never mentioned by the saint's biographer. There are penances, of course, but they are all for open and scandalous sins—never for mere breaches of discipline; and it cannot be said that they erred on the side of severity. A man who had been guilty of fratricide and incest was not too

---

[1] Green, *Short Hist. of the Eng. People*, ch. i. § 3.

harshly dealt with when sentenced to twelve years' exile among the Britons—particularly when it was left quite optional with himself whether the sentence was to be carried out or not.

When we come to the 'Rule' of Columbanus, we are on very different ground. We have none of the genial feasts made for the welcome of visitors; no killing of oxen for the common meal; but day follows day in one monotonous and continued fast, barely enough food for sustaining life being taken, and that consisting merely of vegetables, pulse, meal, and biscuit—only varied by a fast still more strict imposed as a punishment for some paltry offence. Brutal inflictions of the lash are threatened at every step. For speaking in a loud voice there were six stripes. The same punishment for not repressing a cough at the beginning of a psalm, or for omitting to say, Amen. For some offences, as many as two hundred stripes are ordered, to be given twenty-five at a time.

The difference between the two systems is so striking, that a doubt naturally arises in the mind as to whether Columbanus founded his rule on that Comgal after all. There is another possibility: that Bangor was not so very different from Iona, and that Columbanus, being dissatisfied with what he considered its laxity, left it for the purpose of following a stricter rule; and that these terrible whippings are of his own invention. At all events, it is pleasant to remember the picture that Adamnan gives of Iona, which shows us that whatever Bangor may have been, other places in Ireland were very far indeed from accepting such a tyranny as Columbanus would have wished to impose.

This excessive severity, repugnant as it is to all our ideas, was one of the great factors in the success of Columbanus. When carelessness and indifference abounded, the intense earnestness of these men must have been the more remarkable; and when the people thought of religion at all, they could scarcely help being attracted by those to whom the Faith was such a reality that they were ready to give up everything of pleasure and indulgence for its sake.

In the work of Columbanus we have the Irish Church brought for the first time into contact with the outside world. Columba and the monks of Iona, when they invaded Pictland, left the isolation of Ireland for a still greater isolation. Columbanus, on the other hand, found himself surrounded by an ecclesiastical organization in some respects very different from any that he had known at home. The bishops were real spiritual magnates, instead of being, as often in Ireland, subject to the abbot of a monastery. They exercised territorial jurisdiction, and they all of them paid allegiance to the Bishop of Rome. In Ireland, Rome seemed to be a very distant and unknown place; and they had but little conception of that great system of Church government which was being perfected under her auspices.

Columbanus, when he went to France, carried with him all the ideas in which he had been brought up. He never thought of conforming himself to the usages of those into whose land he had come. His monasteries were in Gaul, but they were not Gallic. Whatever was the country in which he sojourned, he was still an Irishman, and it never entered his head that he should belong to any other than the Irish Church.

The differences soon became apparent. Columbanus computed the time for celebrating the feast of

Easter differently from those who were around him, and therefore while one was keeping the fast of Lent, the other was commemorating with a feast the Resurrection of our Lord. Here was a visible token of nonconformity. Any one could see that the Church of Ireland and the Church of France were not in accord. The matter was considered to be of sufficient importance to warrant the assembling of a synod of the French bishops, who considered the advisability of expelling Columbanus from the country. To this synod the latter addressed an epistle, in which he begs that he and his companions may be allowed 'to live with you in peace and charity, in silence amongst these woods, near to the bones of our seventeen brothers who are dead, in the same way as up to the present we have been allowed to live amongst you these twelve years, and that as we have heretofore done, we may still fulfil our duty in praying for you.' He goes on to argue with them the question in dispute, and finally, he makes an appeal for mutual forbearance. But he gives no sign of being ready to alter his practice in the least, or of conforming to the ways of those who were around him. At the same time he wrote a letter to Pope Gregory the Great on the subject. This, as well as another letter written at a later period to Pope Boniface IV., is of the highest importance as throwing light on the position which he took with regard to the Pope, and as telling us from his example something of the way in which the subject of papal supremacy was regarded by the Irish Church. That Columbanus was altogether wrong in his arguments on this particular question, whereas the Church of Rome was right, does not concern the matter one way or the other. At present we have only to consider how far he as a member of the Irish Church considered himself bound by the authority of the Pope.

Columbanus wrote to Pope Gregory in the hope of inducing that pontiff to use his influence for the purpose of quelling the storm that was raging round the Irish missionaries by reason of the opposition of the prelates. He insinuates rather than asserts that the agitation was set on foot by those who did not care to have their evil deeds brought to light, and that many of the bishops had obtained their positions through simony, and therefore were uncanonically ordained. He adduces the authority of Saint Jerome for the Irish practices, and warns the Pope that there ought to be no disagreement between his holiness and the saint, for whoever contradicted the authority of Saint Jerome would be looked upon as a heretic and rejected with scorn by the Churches of the West. He ridicules the idea that the decision made by one pope should in all cases bind his successors. Gregory's predecessor had been Leo, and Columbanus, in a quaint though not very complimentary manner, reminds him that 'a living dog is better than a dead *lion.*'

The letter to Pope Boniface is still more remarkable. He begins it by words which have been often quoted to show that Columbanus of all the fathers uses the strongest language in asserting the Pope's supremacy. He addresses his letter thus: ' To the most renowned Head of all the Churches of all Europe, the most charming Pope, the highly exalted prelate, the pastor of pastors, the most reverend overseer: a humble individual addresses himself to him who is highly exalted, the least to the greatest, a rustic to the polished citizen, a man of feeble utterance to him who is most eloquent; the last speaks to him that is first, the stranger addresses the homeborn, the poorest comes to him who is most mighty: nay, wonderful to relate! a thing never heard of before! that strange bird, the common wood pigeon (Palumbus)[1] dares to write to Father Boniface.'

This paragraph is interesting, as showing that Irishmen in the past, like those in the present, are sometimes disposed to regard the superlative adjective as most important of all the parts of speech. It is certainly an extraordinary introduction for the tirade that follows, in which he unburdens his mind with a vigour of language that is as unique as is the accumulation of compliments with which he begins. He is himself conscious of the fact that what he writes will be distasteful to the authorities at Rome, for at the beginning he endeavours to excuse himself by reminding them that better are the wounds of a friend than the deceitful kisses of an enemy. He then goes on to tell the Pope that 'the name of God is blasphemed among the Gentiles on account of you who are contending, both of you. For I confess, I grieve at the infamy that attaches itself to the chair of Saint Peter.' He gives as his justification of the right to lecture the Pope in this fashion that, 'we Irish—all of us—though we dwell at the very ends of the earth, are disciples of SS. Peter and Paul, and of all the disciples who by the power of the Holy Spirit wrote the Divine Canon. We receive no doctrine beyond that of the Evangelists and Apostles. We have had amongst us no heretic or Jew or schismatic, but the Catholic faith as it was first handed down by you, that is to say, by the successors of the holy apostles, is still kept

---

[1] By way of showing his humility, he will not call himself Columba, 'the dove,' but only Palumbus, 'the wood pigeon.'

by us unshaken.' 'He goes on to tell his holiness that if he desires not to lack apostolic honour he must preserve the apostolic faith. He acknowledges the supremacy of the see of Rome in so far as to give it the *second* place in all the world, Jerusalem being first; but he says that it is a painful and lamentable case if the Catholic faith be not held in the apostolic see; and that under certain circumstances a Church very much younger, but one which has never harboured heretics (in which description he not obscurely designates the Church of Ireland), might sit in judgment on the Church of Rome, and cut it off from communion 'until the memory of the wicked be effaced and consigned to oblivion.'

We are not to suppose that these writings of Columbanus were current in Ireland, or that any one in that country took such a decided stand with regard to the points of controversy. As a matter of fact the question as to the keeping of Easter, which was the subject of the letter to Pope Gregory, had not yet arisen in Ireland, and the 'Controversy of the Three Chapters,' which caused the letter to Pope Boniface, never arose there, and was in all probability quite unknown. The works of Columbanus only show us in what way an Irishman of that age regarded the question of Papal supremacy when brought into close contact with it for the first time. The life of Columbanus brings us down to the beginning of the seventh century (615), and tells us that up to that time the Church of Ireland was independent in so far as to claim the right to interpret for itself the Word of God and ordain its own rites and ceremonies; that it took for its sole rule of faith the writings of the Evangelists and Apostles; that it ignored (and if occasion had arisen would have rejected) papal supremacy ; and that while conscious of its independence and of its difference in some points from the other nations of Christendom, it nevertheless held itself to be a part of the great Catholic Church.

CHAPTER VII.

ASCETICS AND ANCHORITES.

FROM the beginning of the mission of Saint Patrick to the death of Columbanus occupies a period of about two centuries—roughly speaking, the fifth and sixth. The end of that time saw one national Church for Ireland and Scotland, both countries being governed by the same rules, and holding the same doctrines; that is to say, they held the doctrine and discipline of the Church of Gaul as it was at the end of the fourth century. If any development or change had taken place, it must have been brought about independently of any outside influence. It is, therefore, a matter of great interest to the student of general Church history that we should obtain as accurate a picture as possible of the Irish Church in that age. There is perhaps no other way in which we can get as clear an idea of the state of Christendom, for, when changes are taking place, when new developments of doctrine and discipline are being worked out, it is often very difficult to say afterwards how far the process had gone at one particular time. But if at that time there has been a portion separated from the rest, and this portion has continued for centuries isolated, and free from the influences that were producing change elsewhere, we can form a fairly accurate picture of the state of things that existed when the separation took place, by a careful study of the phenomena presented, and an elimination of those peculiarities that are due to merely local causes.

The difference between the rule of Columba and that of Columbanus, which latter may have been founded on that of Comgal, has already been noted. We may hence conclude that in some places a stricter rule was followed than in others, and the conjecture may be hazarded that there was a regular gradation, from simple Christian villages which were called monasteries, but were monastic only in name, to those in which the strictest discipline was observed and the extreme asceticism of the East was more than emulated.

Some countenance to this idea is given by one of an ancient body of canons, attributed to Gildas, who is said to have come to Ireland in the latter part of the sixth century, at the invitation of the chief monarch, for the purpose of restoring ecclesiastical order, 'because all the inhabitants of the island had abandoned the Catholic faith.' This story of the mission of Gildas is discredited by the fact that the period when Ireland is said to have apostatized was in fact one of great spiritual activity, as shown by the works of evangelization undertaken by the different missionaries. But there can be no doubt that the canons are connected with the Irish Church, though probably they belong to a later period. The canon says that 'an abbot who is lax ought not to prohibit his monk from seeking a stricter rule.' Then by way of explanation, it is said, 'monks flying from a lax to a more perfect discipline, and whose abbot is irreligious or immoral and unfit to be admitted to the table of the saints, may be received even without the knowledge of their abbot. But those whose abbot is not excluded from the table of the saints, ought not to be received. How much more those who come from holy abbots, whose only fault is that they possess cattle, and ride in chariots, either from the custom of the country or because of infirmity. For these things are less injurious, if they are possessed in humility and patience, than labouring at the plough, and driving stakes into the earth with presumption and pride.'[1]

From this we may learn not only that some had stricter rules than others, but that there was considerable jealousy between the two classes. Those of lax rule had no sympathy with the stricter ones; and on the other hand the extreme ascetics looked down upon those abbots as unworthy who rode in chariots and had wealth of cattle. It was unavoidable, from the very circumstances of the case, that there should be this diversity. The greatest advocates of monasticism had never dreamt of its becoming the one rule of the Church; but this was the case in Ireland, and therefore it necessarily followed that the system should be modified to meet the circumstances of the case. Extreme asceticism might suit a few enthusiastic souls; but for the ordinary members of the Church, or even of the clergy, it was a yoke which they were not able and could not be expected to bear.

It was not merely in different monasteries that there was this difference in strictness; even in the same establishment the inmates were not all bound by the same rule. A man might become an ascetic without separating himself from his abbot, even though the abbot were one that did not follow a very strict rule himself or impose it on his followers. This brings us to consider the institution of *anchorites*,

---

[1] Quoted from Todd, *Life of St. Patrick*, p. 144.

which forms such a very striking feature in the early Irish Church. These were men who were not contented with the ordinary Christian life, but were supposed to practise greater austerities than those among whom they lived. They dwelt apart, in the 'Desert,' as their portion of the monastery was called.

The name, Desert, recalls to us the fact that the original anchorites were monks of Egypt, who retired into a real desert, for the purpose of spending lives of loneliness and devotion. As far as we are able to judge of them, they presented a not very inviting picture. They were for the most part not only ignorant, but they gloried in their ignorance; they never engaged in any useful work; some of them seem to have laid aside every vestige of civilization and decency; they placed no bounds to their fanaticism; they banished from their hearts every human affection. Though their lives were in one sense examples of extreme self-denial, in another sense they were examples of extreme selfishness. Whatever may be thought of cenobites, or monks living in community, there can only be one opinion about the hermits. They were as a general rule useless and lazy, and under the cloak of humility were filled with spiritual pride.

When the monastic system was introduced into the West, the names were retained, but the things signified were far from being the same. When we speak of the Irish 'anchorites' living in a 'desert,' we must dismiss from our minds nearly all the ideas that we usually connect with these two words. First of all, the anchorites had scarcely one point in common with those of Egypt and Syria. They did not live lives of isolation, but formed part of the community. In later years there were 'enclosed anchorites' found in Ireland. These never left their cells, but spent their whole time each on the grave of his predecessor and with his own grave open beside him. But the old Irish Church was a thing of the past before these made their appearance. They were quite unknown in the period we are now considering. The old Irish anchorites had their duties to perform, like the rest of the monks. In Iona, for example, one of them was a bridge maker. It was not at all uncommon for the anchorite to be abbot of a monastery. Others were bishops, scribes, lawgivers, teachers. Some were even travellers. Of one we are told that he died in Italy.

A good idea of the life they were expected to lead is given us in an ancient 'Rule,' written in Irish, which is attributed to Columba, and belongs, if not to his age, at all events to an early period. Here the religious brother who prefers solitude 'is recommended to reside in contiguity to a principal church, in a secure house with one door, attended by one servant, whose work should be light, where only those should be admitted who converse of God and His Testament, and in special solemnities only. His time was to be spent in prayers for those who received his instructions and for all those who had died in faith, the same as if they had all been his most particular friends. The day was to be divided into three parts, devoted respectively to prayers, good works and reading. The works were to be divided into three parts; the first was to be devoted to his own benefit, in doing what was useful and necessary for his own habitation; the second part to the benefit of the brethren; and the third to the benefit of the neighbours. This last part of his pious works was to consist of precepts or writing, or else sewing clothes or any other profitable industrial work: so that there shall be no idleness, as God says, Thou shalt not appear before Me empty.'[1]

The 'desert' in which these anchorites lived was simply a place set apart for themselves. Sometimes this was near the monastery, as at Glendalough; sometimes it was actually in it, as in the case contemplated by the rule just quoted, and as we know to have been the case at Kells. The desert was a place where penitents might retire for a while and obtain ghostly comfort and advice, for many of the anchorites were famous as *anmcharas*, or 'soul friends.' For the regulation of these, both penitents and advisers, there was an officer appointed, who was called the 'Head of the Desert.'

When these facts are considered, it will be seen that it is most important that we should not be misled by words, when the terms used for the existing circumstances in one country are transferred to those of another. The words, monastery, monk, anchorite, desert, and the like have done more than anything else to give wrong ideas as to what the ancient Irish Church was like. We have seen that in Ireland the anchorite was simply a stricter monk, and when we remember that he was allowed to keep a servant and to receive visitors, we can scarcely say that his rule was too strict. It is very probable, however, that at first no such institutions existed, and that a considerable time elapsed before such a development was thought of. The ancient catalogue

---

[1] O'Curry, *MS. Materials of Anc. Irish Hist.*, p. 374. The last sentence is given in Latin: ' Ut Deus ait: Non apparebis ante me vacuus.' The passage occurs in four places (once in the Apocrypha), but in no case is the Vulgate exactly as here quoted. It will be noticed that the meaning *unemployed* is given to *vacuus*, though the Biblical context requires the meaning *empty-handed*.

of the Irish saints to which reference has been already made tells us that it was the third order of saints who 'used to dwell in desert places, and to live on herbs and water and the alms of the faithful. They despised all earthly things and wholly avoided all whispering and backbiting.' But they were the least holy of the three orders, which shows that asceticism, though it existed at the time, was not regarded as a sign of great sanctity. On the contrary, those were more highly esteemed who needed no such help for the overcoming of sin. The catalogue further tells us that they were later in date than the first order of saints, who established mixed monasteries and had Saint Patrick for their leader. They were later also than the second order, which enforced celibacy, and indeed did not come into existence until the seventh century. That the movement was due to foreign influences is probable, from the fact that while some of them followed the usages of the Irish Church, others conformed to the rules observed by the Continental Churches. This is also borne out by the fact that the Annalists do not chronicle the death of famous anchorites until towards the close of the seventh century.

The conclusion therefore to which we are led is that this institution never at any time had much resemblance to that of the same name in Egypt and elsewhere, and although characteristic of an early age of the Irish Church, was unknown in the very earliest times.

CHAPTER VIII.

THE MINISTRY OF WOMEN.

THE position occupied by women in the ancient Irish Church is a rather difficult, but most interesting subject. In the olden times the women of Ireland were admitted to many employments that are generally regarded as being outside their province. Even in the field of battle they took their place, and it was not until the year 590 that they were exempted from service in the military expeditions. When Tara was in all its glory, the 'barrack of the warlike women' stood within the enclosure, not far from the palace of the king. From the first they played an important part in the history of the Church. They were, as we have seen, admitted freely to the monasteries, or at all events to some of them, and being admitted, they were not always confined to the less important offices. Some of the abbots evidently did not care much for this mixed system. Columba is said to have objected even to cows, giving as his reason, 'where there is a cow there must be a woman, and where there is a woman there must be mischief.' This, by the way, has been triumphantly quoted to show that women were excluded from Iona. But surely it is the very opposite inference that should be drawn. There *were* cows in Iona; therefore, according to Columba, there must have been women.

If the *Lives of the Saints* are to be believed, however, there were some who obstinately excluded women from their communities. In doing so they encountered determined opposition. Kevin of Glendalough is said to have hurled a woman into the lake, because in no other way could he overcome the persistence with which she insisted on obtaining admittance into the monastery. A curious story is also told about Senanus, the saint who has given his name to the River Shannon. He established himself with his followers in an island, and on one occasion a woman sailed across and demanded admission. He met her with a repulse: 'What have women in common with monks? We will not receive thee nor any like thee.' She began to argue with him: 'What! if thou believest that my spirit can receive Jesus Christ, why repulse my body?' But the saint was unmoved by the appeal. 'I believe thee,' he said; 'but no woman shall ever enter here. Go; God save thy soul; but go, return to the world; among us thou wouldest give scandal; thy heart may be chaste, but thy sex is in thy body.' Stories like these could never have taken rise if it had not been a recognised institution at one time for women and men together to form portion of the same community.

In other places they were far from resting contented with such unfriendly exclusion or grudging toleration. They became the instructors of men, and took upon them the training of those who were to be admitted to the priesthood. We read of one who did duty as 'Erenach' at Derry,[1] and who must therefore have transacted all the business of the establishment, superintended the farm opera-

---

[1] *Annals of the Four Masters*, A.D. 1134.

tions, and received the visitors. Of another, we are told that she acted as 'soul friend,' or spiritual adviser to one of the opposite sex. In the Life of Saint Aidan, we are told, 'After Aidan had come to Ireland, he said, I am sorry that I did not ask my instructor who in this island of Ireland should be my soul friend. He was returning to Saint David, walking on the sea, when an angel met him and said, There was great confidence in what thou hast done, in going on foot over the sea. To which Aidan answered, I have not done this through confidence, but through the strength of faith. And the angel said to him, It is not necessary that thou shouldest have a soul friend, for God loves thee, and between thee and God there will be no intermediary one. If, however, thou wishest for a soul friend, thou shalt have Molue, the mother of Choche.'[1] A story like this could never have arisen if it were considered unworthy of a saint to have a woman for his soul friend.

Several instances are recorded of women rising to the highest offices in the Church, and becoming abbesses; that is to say, not mere superiors to communities of women, but heads of establishments formed after the same pattern as the rest, with priests and bishops amongst the inmates, who meekly submitted to the rule of the woman who was the head of the religious 'family.'

The most famous of these abbesses was Bridget, whose monastery at Kildare continued to be famous for many centuries. She was the illegitimate daughter of one of the Irish chiefs, and is said to have been remarkable for her beauty, until, finding it to be an obstacle to her usefulness, she prayed

[1] Rees, *Lives of the Cambro-British Saints.*

that she might be deprived of it; from which time she became remarkably plain. Probably this simply means that she was disfigured by an illness such as small-pox, and was thus led to dedicate herself to a religious life. At all events, she was one of the earliest converts, and for a time became the companion of St. Patrick, whom she accompanied in his preaching tours through the country. Eventually, she founded the monastic establishment at Kildare, which, like the others of that age, consisted of both sexes living together, and bound by the same rules. Having erected her monastery 'on the sure foundations of faith,' it soon became 'the head of nearly all the Irish churches, and the pinnacle towering above all the monasteries of the Scots, whose jurisdiction spread through the whole Hibernian land from sea to sea.'

After a time, she reflected that she ought 'to provide with prudent care regularly in all things for the souls of her people,' and came to the conclusion that 'she could not be without a high priest, to consecrate churches and to settle the ecclesiastical degrees in them.'[1] Accordingly, after a time a bishop, who was also a worker in brass, was admitted to the community; but he became subject to the abbess in the same way as in some other places the bishop was subject to the abbot. Sometimes there was more than one bishop at Kildare. As far as we can judge, the establishment resembled in most respects the ordinary monasteries around them. There was the same entertaining of distinguished strangers and the coming and going of visitors; the same ceremony of washing the feet was observed,

---

[1] See Todd, *Life of St. Patrick*, pp. 11, 12, who here quotes from Cogitosus, *Vita S. Brigidæ*.

only it was done by the sisters instead of by the brothers; the same kind of work, too, went on; the ground was tilled, mechanical arts were pursued, and especially the work of producing illuminated manuscripts occupied a considerable portion of their time. Giraldus Cambrensis gives us a wonderful account of a copy of the Gospels which existed in his time, and which must have been of the same class as the Book of Kells. He tells us that it was miraculously produced. Every night an angel showed the scribe in a dream a copy of the designs he was to execute on the following day, and by the prayers of Bridget he was then enabled to reproduce them. 'In this manner the book was composed, an angel furnishing the designs, Saint Bridget praying, and the scribe copying.'

In later times the abbesses seem to have had less authority, and the establishment was nearly always under the control of some member of the royal family of Leinster, not unfrequently the heir to the throne. A remarkable peculiarity of the monastery at Kildare was the keeping up of a perpetual fire. Giraldus mentions it among the 'Wonders and Miracles of Ireland.' He tells us that 'this fire is surrounded by a hedge, made of stakes and brushwood, and forming a circle, within which no male can enter; and if any one should presume to enter, which has been sometimes attempted by rash men, he will not escape the Divine vengeance. Moreover, it is only lawful for women to blow the fire, fanning it or using bellows only, and not with their breath.' There has been much speculation as to the meaning of this fire, but its origin is lost in mystery, and is not improbably to be traced to the old Druidism. Henry de Londres, one of the Anglo-Norman archbishops of Dublin, believing it to be of idolatrous origin, caused it to be extinguished in 1220, but it was again relighted, and continued until the time of the dissolution of the monasteries in the reign of Henry VIII. It furnishes us with an example of how the old Celtic usages were often tolerated by the Romish party when they could not be abolished.

There were many establishments in Ireland which owed their origin to Kildare. Saint Bridget's influence, we are told, 'like a fruitful vine, spreading all around with growing branches,' extended itself through the whole country. But their record seems, for the most part, to have perished. In a few places we read of abbesses, as for example in Clonburren on the Shannon, and Clonbroney in the County Longford. The latter was founded in the year 734 by Samthann, who was a poetess, and who is herself celebrated in verse by the literary king, Hugh Allen. He writes concerning her:

> 'Samthann for enlightening various sinners,
> A servant who observed stern chastity,
> In the northern plain of fertile Meath
> Great suffering did Samthann endure.
> She undertook a thing not easy,
> Fasting for the kingdom above,
> She lived on scanty food,
> Hard were her girdles.
> She struggled in venomous conflicts,
> True was her heart amid the wicked;
> To the bosom of the Lord, with a pure death
> Samthann passed from her sufferings.'[1]

It is not quite clear whether there were other establishments in Ireland where both sexes were united under the rule of the abbess, as at Kildare.

---

[1] *Annals of the Four Masters*, A.D. 734.

But it is certain that in England and on the continent there were many like it, where Irish, or at all events Celtic, teachers had made their influence felt. In France, for example, Saint Fara's monastery at Brie followed at first the Rule of Saint Columbanus. Earcongota, daughter of Earconbert, King of Kent, and her kinswoman Ethelberga, were inmates, and the latter was at one time abbess. But the establishment included brethren as well as sisters, for when Earcongota died, 'many of the brethren of that monastery that were in the other houses declared that they had then plainly heard concerts of angels singing, and the noise as it were of a multitude entering the monastery.'[1]

The famous Saint Hilda presided over such a monastery at Whitby in Yorkshire, and was in her day the upholder of Irish customs, although at the time the Roman missionaries in England were using all their influence against them.[2] She had been converted by Paulinus, first bishop of the Northumbrians, but had received most of her religious education from Saint Aidan, who came forth from Iona. She was strict in her discipline, and insisted on community of goods, 'so that after the example of the primitive Church no person was there rich, and none poor, all being in common to all, and none having any property.' 'She obliged those who were under her direction to attend so much to the reading of the Holy Scriptures, and to exercise themselves so much in works of justice, that many might be there found fit for ecclesiastical duties, and to serve at the altar.' In this way she trained a large number for the sacred ministry, of whom no less than five became bishops. She seems to have been

[1] Bede, *Eccl. Hist.*, iii. 8. [2] *Ib.*, iii. 25.

not only a ruler, but a preacher, for we are told that notwithstanding sickness, she never failed 'publicly and privately to instruct the flock committed to her charge.'[1]

Among those who acknowledged her as abbess was one whose name has come down to us as the first of the Anglo-Saxon writers, Cædmon, whose Metrical Paraphrase of Holy Scripture is not only a monument of literature, but presents us with the earliest attempt to translate the Bible into the vulgar language of the people.[2] Bede tells us that 'he sang the creation of the world, the origin of man, and all the history of Genesis: and made verses on the departure of the children of Israel out of Egypt, and their entering into the land of promise, with many other histories from Holy Writ; the Incarnation, Passion, Resurrection of our Lord, and His Ascension into heaven; the coming of the Holy Ghost, and the preaching of the Apostles; also the terror of future judgment, the horror of the pains of hell, and the delights of heaven; besides many more about the Divine benefits and judgments, by which he endeavoured to turn away all men from the love of vice, and to excite in them the love of and application to good actions; for he was a very religious man, humbly submissive to regular discipline, but full of zeal against those who behaved themselves otherwise; for which reason he ended his life happily.'

A branch of Hilda's establishment was founded thirteen miles from Whitby, and again a lady was placed at the head of it, Saint Bega, from Ireland, who is still commemorated by the name Saint Bees, which the place bears at the present day, and where in the well-known Theological College the same

---

[1] Bede, *Eccl. Hist.*, iv. 23.   [2] *Ib.* iv., 24.

work of training candidates for Holy Orders is now carried on. At Barking, Coldingham and Watton there were monasteries conducted on similar principles. The arrangement does not seem to have struck the Venerable Bede as incongruous or extraordinary, although he does relate some not very creditable incidents, which show that in some cases at least the system produced those evils which, on *a priori* grounds, one might expect would have destroyed it before a generation had passed. For example, one of the monks of Coldingham had, he tells us, a vision of an angel, who said to him, 'I having now visited all this monastery regularly, have looked into every one's chambers and beds, and found none of them except yourself busy about the care of his soul; but all of them, both men and women, either indulge themselves in slothful sleep, or are awake in order to commit sin; for even the cells that were built for praying or reading are now converted into places of feasting, drinking, talking, and other delights; the very virgins dedicated to God laying aside the respect due to their profession, whensoever they are at leisure, apply themselves to wearing fine garments, either to use in adorning themselves like brides, to the danger of their condition, or to gain the friendship of strange men; for which reason a heavy judgment from heaven is deservedly ready to fall on this place and its inhabitants by devouring fire.'[1] The result of this warning was a temporary reformation, but after a time, relaxing again into their former habits, the judgment threatened came upon them, and a fire destroyed the whole monastery.

All these English establishments, which were

---

[1] Bede, *Eccl. Hist.*, iv. 25.

under the control of women, were founded by those who were of Irish origin, or had come under Irish influence. One may therefore conclude that this institution of the mixed monastery was one peculiar to the ancient Celtic Church, and that the position occupied by women was one of greater importance than was the case in any other country.

CHAPTER IX.

CHURCH OFFICERS PECULIAR TO IRELAND.

In order to complete the description of the peculiarities of the Irish Church, a few words must be said on some Church officers which seem to have been found only in Ireland.

The head of every monastery is sometimes called the abbot of the place, but still more frequently he is designated the Coarb of the founder. This title arose from the tribal organization. Coarb means *inheritor* or *successor*. Thus, the Abbot of Iona was Coarb of Columkill. The same title would be taken by the Abbot of Derry, or Kells, or Swords, or of any other Columban monastery. The Abbot of Clonmacnois was Coarb of Kerian; the Abbot of Armagh was Coarb of Patrick; and similarly, the head of every establishment was called after the first founder. Sometimes the head of the chief community of any order was called Arch-Coarb. This signified that he was the inheritor not only of the tribal rights of the founder, but that he had also authority over all the lesser places where the same rule was followed. Thus the idea of succession rather than of locality was that which was prominent in their minds. In other countries, the opposite rule held. The names of our own parishes and dioceses, for example, are simple territorial distinctions, and have no suggestion in them of each ecclesiastic carrying on the work begun by his predecessors. In Ireland, however, not only was this idea of inheritance kept in view, but they seem to have thought that other Churches were all formed on the same model. Even the Pope is spoken of as Abbot of Rome and Coarb of Peter, as if he were the head of an establishment in Rome similar in character to one of the monastic schools of Ireland. The Coarbs were elected in the same manner as the secular chieftains. Chiefs and kings obtained their positions by election, but the hereditary principle was so far recognised that no one could be elected who did not belong to the ruling family. In the same manner, every member of the community had his voice in the election of coarb, but was restricted in his choice to one of the family of the founder.

The community itself was generally called a 'family.' We have this term used as late as the year 1203, when the 'family of Derry' went over to help the 'family of Iona' in one of their disputes. Here again, it is needless to remark, we have the system of clanship showing itself. Every tribe was regarded as a family bearing the name of its first chief, and in the same way every religious establishment was a family bearing the name of its first founder.

The business affairs of the brotherhood were in the hands of the *Erenach* and the *Economist*. The former, who is often erroneously called an Archdeacon by those who forget that such an office was unknown in the ancient Irish Church, used to manage the outlying farms, which were sometimes let to *beytaghs* or Church tenants. They were the dispensers of hospitality, and in some cases distributed the alms of the community. The economist apportioned his work to each inmate of the monastery, and was bursar and general business man. He was not always a popular officer. When a brother was fond of reading and study, he did not care to be sent off to cut timber or engage in farm work. The economist, however, had to be obeyed, and no one was allowed to shirk his share of the manual labour.

The *Anmchara* or 'soul friend' was one of the most remarkable institutions of the Irish Church. It has been often assumed that the office was simply that of confessor, and its existence has been appealed to as showing that auricular confession and priestly absolution were both practised in the early Irish Church. Such a view is reduced to an absurdity by the story already given about Saint Aidan. When his life was written it was not considered impossible that the office should be held by a woman. And all that we know of soul friends leads us to the same conclusion. They were advisers, not confessors; and they gave guidance and direction, not absolution. It is highly probable that Irish teachers of that age would have called Deborah the soul friend of Barak. The position she occupied was exactly that which the soul friends of old occupied. A few examples will be the best way of explaining the kind of service that they rendered.

After the battle of Cooldreeny, and when Columba had been excommunicated by the Synod of Teltown, he sought his soul friend for advice, and it was he who suggested the missionary work which was begun and set forward in Iona.

We have another example in the life of Fintan or Munna, founder of Taghmon in the County Wexford. He was one of the many visitors at Iona, and arrived there shortly after the death of Columba. To journey as far as Iona had long been the great desire of his life, and one would have thought that the undertaking was not of such tremendous magnitude but that he might fairly have made the journey on his own responsibility. He, however, thought it better first to have recourse to his soul friend, Colum Crag, and 'take advice from his better counsel'; and it was only when he had 'laid his mind open to him,' and had received his consent and encouragement, that he began the journey. We are told that as the two were discussing the matter together, some of the brethren from Iona arrived. On being asked about their journey, they answered, 'We have lately landed from Britain, and this day we have come from Derry.' 'Is your holy father, Columba, well?' asked Colum Crag. But they, bursting into tears, exclaimed with great sorrow, 'The patron is indeed well, for a few days ago he departed to Christ.'[1]

Another interesting example of a soul friend having been consulted is given in an old manuscript, at present in the library of Trinity College, Dublin. One of the minor kings, Fiacha by name, who lived in the middle of the seventh century, was killed by his own people, and his brother Donnchadh 'came upon them in revenge; but he stayed his vengeance until he should consult his soul friend, the Coarb of Saint Columkill, to whom he sent a message to Iona, to ask his advice on the case.' The answer, brought back by two confidential clerics, was a strange one. Donnchadh was advised 'to send sixty couples of the men and women of the offending tribe in boats out upon the sea, and then leave them to the judgment of God. The exiles were accordingly put into small boats, launched upon the water, and watched so that they should not land again.' A curious development of the story is that the 'two confidential clerics,'

---

[1] Adamnan, *Life of Columba*, i. 2.

instead of going back to their abbot, as of course they would have done if vows of obedience were then in force, 'determined to go of their own will on a wandering pilgrimage,' and eventually followed the fortunes of the castaways, who had landed safely on an island.[1]

A very remarkable 'soul friend' was Maelsuthain O'Carroll, who lived in the early years of the eleventh century. He was himself a chief, and for a great part of his life had lived as an ordinary petty king. In his later years, however, he was an inmate of the abbey at Innisfallen, in one of the Lakes of Killarney, and became soul friend to the famous Brian Boru. The Four Masters tell us that he was chief doctor of the Western world in his time, and that he died after a good life. His handwriting is still to be seen in the Book of Armagh. He was manifestly a very learned man, and seems to have been employed as scribe and historian by Brian Boru. Being a man of the world, he may well also have been adviser as to matters of state. But with regard to the good life with which the Annalists credit him, the evidence seems to be all the other way. His immoralities were notorious—so much so, that it is difficult to see how he could have been soul friend with spiritual advantage to any one.

In many ways there is considerable resemblance between the soul friends and some of the prophets of whom we read in the Old Testament. They were, it is true, quite unlike such men as Elijah and Isaiah and Jeremiah, but they were consulted much in the same way as Nathan was consulted by David and Micaiah by Ahab and Jehoshaphat. Like Samuel, they sometimes suggested that a war should be

---

[1] O'Curry, *MS. Materials of Anc. Irish Hist.*, p. 333.

undertaken, and at one time it seems almost to have become a rule not to engage in battle until their opinion as to the merits of the contest had been obtained. In the story of the battle of Kilmashoge, as related by the Four Masters under the year 917, the soul friend plays much the same part as would have been taken by one of the old Hebrew prophets. The Irish leader, Neal Glunduff, was incited to attack the Danish invaders by his soul friend, who prophesied victory, accompanied the army into the field, and when the fortunes of war were going against his countrymen, refused to give Neal a horse to carry him away from the battle.

All these instances, and many more that might be quoted, show us how different the soul friend was from a confessor. The office was simply what the name implied, and was very far indeed from carrying with it the ideas of auricular confession and priestly absolution. As an example of the kind of confession that was really practised in the Irish Church, and the doctrine of absolution that was preached, we may take the story of Fechnus, as related by Adamnan: 'He (Fechnus) confessed his sins in the presence of all who were there. The saint then, shedding tears likewise, said to him, "Arise, my son, and be comforted. The sins which thou hast committed are forgiven, because, as it is written, a contrite and humble heart God does not despise."'[1]

It is a question of considerable difficulty to determine how far the ancient Irish Church succeeded in making its influence felt on the people in general. The monastic form, while in one way a source of

---

[1] Adamnan, *Life of Columba*, i. 30. The verse from Psalm li. 17, as here quoted, differs from the Vulgate in having *spernit* instead of *despicies*.

strength, because it joined men together in a holy brotherhood, yet was in another way a source of weakness, since it left those who were outside bereft to some extent of that leaven of goodness which the presence of even a few earnest and good men would have given them. The battles which were waged continually between the different tribes would make us suspect that the Gospel of peace had made but small progress in melting the hearts of the barbarian warriors; and when we find the Christian communities also joining at times in the fray, we are almost ready to conclude that the Church itself was corrupt, and had altogether failed in its mission. It is a subject, however, on which mistakes may easily be made. Many of the old battles that are duly recorded by the Annalists, would now be regarded as mere faction fights, and are only magnified by their antiquity into acts of national warfare. It must always be remembered, too, that much of the disorder of the age is due to the system of government. When a small country is divided into a large number of independent or semi-independent kingdoms, it is almost certain to have wars and fightings without end. Even the personal loyalty of the subjects, though an estimable quality in itself, would only help the disorder, because it made them ready to follow their leader in blind obedience, making his quarrel their own, without pausing to enquire as to the rights and wrongs of the question.

On the other hand, the Church was in many cases the helper of the weak, the asylum of the fugitive, the arbiter of justice. As an illustration of how the Church interposed at times to secure justice between the different tribes, we may take the case of what was called the Boromean tribute. This was a tribute of cows which the King of Leinster was required to pay every third year to the monarch of Ireland. It was originally imposed in the first century of our era, as a punishment for the disgraceful conduct of the King of Leinster at that time. But for centuries afterwards it was exacted, and was from time to time the fruitful cause of war and bloodshed. The injustice of continuing the imposition for an offence personal in the first instance, and committed so long in the past, seems never to have been considered, until the matter was taken up in the latter part of the seventh century by Saint Moling, who had founded a monastery in the County Carlow. This Leinster Christian effected what the Leinster armies were unable to accomplish. He brought the monarch to see that the tax was unjust, and ought to be abolished. Accordingly Finachta the Festive, in the year 680, decreed that the tribute would be no longer required, and thus what had been the cause of more civil war than anything else in the whole history of the nation, came to an end. Strange to say, when the king on this occasion consulted his soul friend, he was advised by him to continue the tax; but happily he had enough good sense to disregard the evil advice, and do that which was just and right. This was all the more remarkable, as the ecclesiastic whose guidance he followed belonged to the tribe of his enemies.

A powerful weapon in the hands of the Church, and one not unfrequently employed, was what may be called the 'ecclesiastical curse.' The most remarkable instance in which this was used was the case of the royal palace and city of Tara, and it will illustrate well the great power which it enabled the Church to wield. The king, Dermot—the same monarch who fought with Saint Columba—took prisoner and afterwards condemned to death a brother of Saint Ruan of Lorrha, in the County Tipperary. The judgment was unjust, and the cause was warmly taken up by the prisoner's saintly kinsman. But reasoning and entreaty were alike in vain, and the sentence was carried out. Saint Ruan immediately repaired to Tara, and 'laid his curse upon it'; the result being that the whole place was deserted, the Feast of Tara, which was one of the national institutions, was discontinued, and it ceased from that time to be the royal residence.

It must have been this institution of the ecclesiastical curse that Giraldus Cambrensis had in his mind when he penned the curious chapter in which he sets forth how the saints of Ireland appear to be of a vindictive temper. The explanation that he gives is a remarkable one, and is perhaps worth quoting in this place. 'As the Irish people,' he says, ' possessed no castles, while the country is full of marauders who live by plunder, the people, and more especially the ecclesiastics, made it their practice to have recourse to the churches, instead of fortified places, as refuges for themselves and their property; and by Divine Providence and permission, there was frequent need that the Church should visit her enemies with the severest chastisements; this being the only mode by which evil-doers and impious men could be deterred from breaking the peace of ecclesiastical societies, and for securing even to a servile submission the reverence due to the very churches themselves from a rude and irreligious people.'[1]

Finally, it deserves to be noticed, as bearing on the influence of the Church, that it was a very usual thing for kings and other great men, after having

---

[1] Giraldus Camb., *Top. Hib.*, ii. 55.

spent the greater part of their life in warfare and in managing the affairs of state, to retire at length and finish their days in one of the monasteries. Though thus retired from the world, they would be far from losing their influence. The young king would naturally consult his father in cases of emergency; the youthful warriors would take counsel with those who had been the leaders of a former generation, and this would be in many instances almost the same as taking counsel with the abbot and bishop, so that the influence of the Church would be very powerful indeed. How much in this way it moderated violent passions, and promoted the cause of justice and goodness, it is not easy for us now to estimate; but the Church which has left such an excellent record as a missionary organization, and in which the Word of God was so much studied and honoured and prized, cannot have been other than a great power for goodness. We shall hereafter see how it promoted art and learning and civilization to an extent that we would never have imagined if we only thought of the barbarism and lawlessness which overspread the country at a later age.

CHAPTER X.

AUGUSTINE OF CANTERBURY AND THE IRISH CHURCH.[1]

We have now to consider how the Irish Church came to be moulded by exterior influences. Up to the present our attention has been confined to such developments as took place independently. The Irish Church, as we have seen, stood alone beyond the reach of the revolutions and controversies that produced such changes in other parts of Christendom. It is a remarkable fact that it was her own missionary enterprise that first brought her within the sphere of foreign influence. The peculiarities of the Irish Church were well known. Columbanus and other Irish travellers had, in most countries of Europe, founded institutions which were formed after the model of those at home. The points in which they differed from those around them furnished subjects for discussion to popes and synods, but no effort seems to have been made to influence Ireland itself, or bring it into conformity with the other Western countries. It was only when in England the Irish missionaries met those who had been sent from Rome, and absolutely refused to regard them as other than heretical, that any action was taken; and even then it was anything but effectual. In regard to the particular matter — the Paschal controversy — which was first in dispute, it was the influence of native scholars and travellers that at length prevailed, and the concessions that were made, were made on account of the arguments brought forward by them, and not in deference to any exterior authority.

We shall first see how the Romish and Irish ecclesiastics were brought into contact, and we will then consider the differences which made themselves at once apparent.

The Saxons first landed in England in the year 449, after which date they continued to arrive in successive immigrations, until they had occupied a great part of the country. It was not until a century and a half later that any serious effort was made for their conversion. In the meantime they had driven the Britons before them, had destroyed the churches, and had set up the worship of Woden and Thor where the name of Christ had formerly been invoked. When Pope Gregory the Great was as yet but a deacon in Rome, he had a great desire to dedicate himself to the work of evangelizing this nation. But the obstacles raised by admiring friends, who desired to retain him in their midst, prevented him from carrying his purpose into effect, and it was only after his elevation to the papal chair that he found another who possessed the same enthusiasm, and was ready to undertake what must have seemed at the time to be a hazardous enterprise.

The mission of Augustine of Canterbury, to whom this work was committed by Pope Gregory, is an event with which all readers of English history are familiar, and its story need not be repeated here. The older historians have for the most part assumed that English Christianity was all the result of this mission from Rome. It is now recognised that such a view is quite erroneous. The work of Augustine was confined to the southern part of the country, and even there his success was more apparent than real, and has been magnified by succeeding writers, who considered it a matter of conscience to ignore or disparage any missionary effort that did not draw its inspiration from the Church of Rome. The whole enterprise depended on the enthusiasm of the one man. The companions of Augustine were reluctant in entering upon the work; they had scarcely put their hand to the plough when they wanted to turn back; and they were ready to desert it as soon as he was dead. Then, the great majority of the converts were Christians only in name. The preachers, acting under the advice of the Pope, made every possible concession to idolatry. The idol temples for example were retained; and, when dedicated to Christian worship, the people were encouraged to make feasts beside them, in the same way as they used to do in celebrating the sacrificial rites of heathenism.

The result was that when Augustine died, and the missionary enterprise passed into the hands of less enthusiastic workers, nearly the whole nation relapsed into idolatry.

The British Church—now confined to the western parts of the country—held itself sullenly aloof from the work of evangelization. Augustine rightly regarded this as a dereliction of duty, and made overtures to them, in hopes that they might be brought to recognise their obligation in this respect, and would join with him in the common labour of preaching the Gospel to the Gentiles. He made arrangements for assembling a synod, which was to consist of both parties, at a place still called in the time of Bede, Augustine's Ac, that is of Augustine's Oak. Up to that time both he and his party had held the Britons and Irish in great esteem for sanctity, being, it would seem, quite unaware that their usages differed in any wise from those to which they had been accustomed in Rome. No sooner, however, was the synod assembled, than the differences made themselves at once apparent, and the party separated without coming to any conclusion.

A second meeting was arranged, and in the meantime the British delegates took counsel with an anchorite, celebrated for his wisdom, who advised them to be led by Augustine, if he were a man of God. On being asked how they were to know this, the anchorite replied, that if he were a man of God he would be meek and humble, and would show his humility by rising up to greet them when they arrived at the synod. Unfortunately Augustine failed in the test. The Britons designedly came late, in order that Augustine, being already seated, should have the opportunity of rising up at their approach; but he continued sitting in his chair, and the British delegates, observing this, were in a passion, charged him with pride, and endeavoured to contradict all that he said.[1]

The British Church was in doctrine and discipline almost identical with the Church of Ireland; but the Roman missionaries were not aware of this fact, and were hoping better things from the Irish.[2] They learned, however, from Columbanus in France, that Irish and Britons were both alike, and when at length they did actually come in contact with an Irish bishop, he absolutely refused to join in their communion, and expressed his hostility not only by refusing to eat with them, but even to take his repast in the same house as that in which they were

---

[1] Bede, *Eccl. Hist.*, ii. 2.   [2] *Ib.*, ii. 4.

entertained. This looks like a display of temper; yet, strange to say, this bishop (Saint Dagan) is said by Irish authorities to have been remarkable for his meekness.[1] Probably he considered that eating under the same roof with them would be equivalent to the making of a league.

In one respect the Britons and the Irish were very different. The former had carried their hate of the Saxons so far as to deliberately withhold from them any knowledge of the Christian religion. 'We will not preach the faith,' they said, 'to the cruel race of strangers who have treacherously driven our ancestors from their country, and robbed their posterity of their inheritance.' The Irish, on the other hand, were in the full enthusiasm of missionary enterprise; their labours among the Picts had been crowned with a brilliant success, and they now began a similar work in the north of England.

Oswald, King of Northumbria, had once as a refugee been hospitably entertained in the island of Iona. When he found himself with the reins of government in his hands, he asked that a teacher should come from thence to instruct his people in the religion of Christ. Bishop Corman, who was first sent, met with no success, and soon returned, reporting that he had not been able to do any good to the nation he had been sent to preach to, because they were uncivilized men, and of a stubborn and barbarous disposition. A young man in the assembly, hearing this report, gave a gentle rebuke to the disheartened labourer. 'I am of opinion, brother,' said he, 'that you were more severe to your unlearned hearers than you ought to have

---

[1] See Card. Moran, *Irish Saints in Great Britain*, p. 211.

been, and did not at first, conformably to the apostolic rule, give them the milk of more easy doctrine, till being by degrees nourished with the Word of God they should be capable of greater perfection and be able to practise God's sublimer precepts.'[1] This sentiment seemed to contain so much wisdom that the speaker, Saint Aidan, was at once fixed upon as the fittest for the work. He accordingly set out, accompanied by some companions like-minded with himself. They were favourably received by King Oswald, who allowed them to choose for themselves a site on which to found their first establishment. They, taking Iona as their model, chose the small island of Lindisfarne, in which they reproduced as nearly as possible the different features of the parent monastery. Their work, prosecuted as it was with vigour and tempered with wisdom and prudence, was eminently successful, and the whole nation was brought to the obedience of the faith. Lindisfarne became in the very best sense a second Iona. In the meantime some of the faint-hearted in the Roman mission, becoming ashamed of their cowardice, had returned to the conflict; new helpers had joined them, and they began to build up again the Church which had been so suddenly destroyed. The result of all was that Saxon England had two Churches: one in the south in communion with the Church of Rome, and one in the north in communion with the Church of Ireland. When these two parties met, the isolation of the Irish Church was for the first time broken, and the differences between it and the Church of Rome became at once apparent.

Let us now ask what these differences were.

---

[1] Bede, *Eccl. Hist.*, iii. 5.

CHAPTER XI.

POINTS OF DIFFERENCE BETWEEN IRELAND AND ROME.

THE first and most important difference that showed itself when the Roman missionaries in England and the Irish Church came into contact was, that the former were subject to the Pope, whereas the latter was not. This has been denied by some, but the proof of it is simply overwhelming. Every point of ritual, unimportant in itself, in which the Irish refused to conform to the Romans goes to show that this difference existed. In all their discussions it is tacitly assumed. The favourite argument of the Romans is that they are followers of Saint Peter, an honour which they altogether deny to their opponents. The Irish consider it a sufficient reply that they follow Saint John, or even Saint Columba. On one famous occasion a decision was given against the Irish, not on the merits of the question, but because the one side could quote the verse, 'Thou art Peter, and upon this rock I will build My Church, and the gates of hell shall not prevail against it. And I will give unto thee the keys of the kingdom of heaven'; whereas the other side could show nothing of the same kind about Columba. Such a way of deciding the question would have been impossible if both sides acknowledged equally the supremacy of the see of Rome. Then, the ignorance which the

Romans display concerning Ireland and everything Irish, shows that whatever theory may have been held in papal circles as to the subjection of all other Churches, as a matter of *fact* Ireland had been left to go its own way without any assertion of authority on the part of the Pope. Augustine and they who were with him never knew until they were in Britain that the British Church was different from their own; and when they were made painfully conscious of this fact, they still thought that the Irish must be like themselves. Finally, the fact that they denied the validity of the Irish ordinations is the clearest possible proof that in their eyes at all events the Church of Ireland was not in communion with Rome.

It is of no avail to bring forward, as is often done, the many points of agreement between Rome and Ireland. That the two Churches did agree in many, nay, in most points, is historically certain, and it would be a mistake to represent the Irish Church as being in all respects like the Protestants of to-day. But, just as the Churches of the East and West at the time when they were not only independent, but hostile, were yet in agreement on every fundamental doctrine, so the Irish Church, though it differed from the Church of Rome only on those points in which Rome of the seventh century differed from Rome of the fifth, yet owed no allegiance to the papal see, and does not seem to have been conscious of the fact that Rome had already made a universal demand for such allegiance.

A less important, but more striking difference between the two Churches, was the method of computing the time for holding the festival of Easter. Easter is always held on the first Sunday after the fourteenth day of the first Jewish month. As the

Jewish months follow the moon, the feast necessarily comes each year at a different period, and in order to calculate this time correctly a computation is made of the number of years after which the moons will come on exactly the same days as before. This term of years is called a 'cycle.' If in any year Easter falls say on the last day of March, it will again fall on that day when the number of years in the cycle have gone by. The calculation requires a considerable amount of astronomical knowledge, and a great many different numbers have been proposed. The Metonic cycle, called after its inventor Meton of Athens (B.C. 432), was a period of nineteen years. The Jewish cycle, followed by the early Christians, was one of eighty-four years. The famous Hippolytus (A.D. 230) proposed a cycle of one hundred and twelve years. The Alexandrians, after the Council of Nicæa, fell back on the old Metonic cycle of nineteen years; but their adhesion to it was not constant. Theophilus of Alexandria (A.D. 380) proposed a cycle of four hundred and thirty-seven years, and Cyril of Alexandria (A.D. 412), one of ninety-five years. Meantime the Church of Rome had mostly followed the eighty-four year period, sometimes called the cycle of Anatolius (A.D. 284), although really of much older date than his time. Finally a cycle of five hundred and thirty-two years was proposed by Victorius (A.D. 463), and this in the end received general acceptance. It is now generally known as the cycle of Dionysius Exiguus (A.D. 527), and is practically the cycle used at the present day.

When Christianity was first preached in Ireland the eighty-four year cycle of Anatolius was in use. The Irish Church therefore continued to use it, and when the Church of Rome changed it for a better and more accurate computation, Ireland was unconscious of the change, and continued in the old way. They also followed the rule that when the fourteenth moon fell on a Sunday, Easter might be kept on that day, whereas the Romans, following the Nicene canon, held that it should not be kept until the Sunday following. The matter involved no doctrine, except indirectly the authority of Rome; but as it led to the keeping of the great Christian feast at different times—the two computations sometimes differing by nearly a month—it was a diversity of use that was very apparent, and prevented union in worship more than other differences of much greater importance would have done.

When the matter came to be argued there was an astonishing amount of ignorance or dishonesty displayed. For example, the Roman missionaries charged the Irish with the quartadeciman heresy, This was either a mistake or a misrepresentation. The quartadeciman controversy was, it is true, about the time when the feast of Easter ought to be held, but it had no concern as to the particular cycle which should be employed. The Romans also boldly claimed the authority of Saint Peter for the cycle first put forward by Victorius in the year 463. The Irish, on their part, claimed the authority of Saint John for the cycle of Anatolius. In this they probably were partly right. It is very likely that this was the cycle actually used by Saint John; but the subject is one on which we have little authentic information.

It may seem strange to us that a question like this, which after all was astronomical rather than theological, could have been regarded as of such immense importance. But when we remember how often some outward act, indifferent in itself, may become the way of expressing belief in a particular doctrine, we can easily see that the controversy may, after all, have been as important as it was most certainly believed to be by both sides that took part in it. The difference between the two words *homoousios* and *homoiousios* may seem insignificant, yet underlying it was the great question which convulsed the whole Church at the time of the Arian controversy. In our own day it may seem a paltry subject of dispute whether a clergyman should stand at the side or end of the holy table; yet it becomes quite different when the posture comes to be regarded as the outward expression of doctrine. In somewhat the same way this Easter controversy was regarded. It was the visible method of declaring to which Church a man belonged. As Bede says of Saint Aidan, 'He could not keep Easter contrary to the customs of those who had sent him.'[1] In other words, this was his method of declaring that he owed his allegiance to the Church of Iona, and not to the Church of Rome.

Another difference, unimportant in itself, but zealously clung to for the same reason, was the tonsure. The practice of shaving the head in token of dedication to God was found among some heathen nations, and was not unknown among the Jews. It was introduced into the Christian Church in connection with monasticism. In the Eastern Church the tonsure consisted in shaving the whole head; in the Western, only the top of the head was shaved, leaving a circle of hair which was supposed to have a resemblance to the crown of thorns. The Celtic tonsure differed from both, and consisted in shaving

---

[1] Bede, *Eccl. Hist.*, iii. 25.

the front of the head in a line from ear to ear. The origin of this curious custom has not as yet been satisfactorily investigated, nor is it possible for us now to say whence this Celtic tonsure was derived. But it will be easily understood how a peculiarity of this kind is clung to, when it becomes the badge of a party. History furnishes us with numberless examples in which some particular way of cutting the hair, some peculiarity in dress, some simple ornament, the wearing of one particular colour or of some flower, has been adopted as the distinguishing mark of a religious or political party, and has been at once raised to an importance that it would not otherwise possess. It has given zealous men an opportunity of displaying their zeal, it has compelled time-servers and waverers to declare themselves, it has shown the strength of the party, and for these reasons has been clung to with the greatest devotion. The white and red roses of York and Lancaster—the cropped hair of the Roundheads and the flowing locks of the Cavaliers—the broad-brimmed hats, poke bonnets, and sombre grey of the Quakers—the orange and blue of the Revolution—are all cases in point. In the same way the Celtic tonsure was regarded by the Irish as the outward mark of their ecclesiastical independence, and for that reason was zealously preserved.

Of more importance was the question of ordination; but unfortunately we cannot now say in what the difference between the two Churches consisted. Bishops among the Irish were consecrated by a single bishop, whereas among the Romans there were ordinarily three employed. But the rule was not a strict one. When Augustine of Canterbury asked the question, whether a bishop might be ordained by him without other bishops being present,

Pope Gregory answers, 'As for the Church of England, in which you are as yet the only bishop, you can no otherwise ordain a bishop than in the absence of other bishops.' It is evident therefore that this of itself would not have rendered the Irish ordinations invalid in the sight of Rome. Yet it is quite clear that they were so regarded. The very answer of Pope Gregory shows it, for he completely ignores the bishops of the British and Irish Churches who were already in the country. According to modern Romish doctrine, the sacrament of orders cannot be repeated; yet we find that re-ordination was insisted on in the case of Celtic bishops.

Let us take, for example, the case of Saint Chad. When he was first consecrated bishop, the ceremony was performed by Wini, Bishop of the West Saxons, assisted by two British bishops who kept Easter according to the Roman method, 'for at that time,' Bede informs us, 'there was no other bishop canonically ordained besides that Wini'—that is to say, the British and Irish were all regarded as outside the pale of the Church of Rome. Here we have the canonical number of consecrators, and one of them at least had orders which were recognised by the Church of Rome; but the form used on the occasion must have been the Celtic, for Archbishop Theodore of Canterbury afterwards upbraided Bishop Chad, that he had not been duly consecrated, and himself 'completed his ordination after the Catholic manner.'[1] Chad had received his religious training from the Irish, and in his youthful days had spent some years in Ireland; for a long time, too, he had upheld the Celtic customs against the teachings of

---

[1] Bede, *Eccl. Hist.*, iv. 2.

Rome; but at length, becoming a convert, he had experiences curiously similar to those with which the men who have followed his footsteps in more modern times have been made familiar.

That this was not the mere excess of zeal of one particular archbishop, is shown by the fact that one of the canons of the old Anglo-Saxon Church enacts, 'That such as have received ordination from the bishops of the Irish or Britons who in the matter of Easter and the tonsure are not united to the Catholic Church, must again by imposition of hands be confirmed by a Catholic bishop.' It is probable that the Irish on their part behaved similarly towards any that came from the Romish party to them. We have no record as to how they dealt with ecclesiastics, but ordinary people leaving the 'Catholic party' had to undergo a forty days' penance before the Celts would receive them.

On the subject of the celibacy of the clergy we must speak with less confidence, as the evidence is to some extent conflicting. When Saint Patrick's mission began celibacy was highly esteemed in Gaul and Western Europe, but was not universally imposed on the clergy; and this seems exactly to represent the state of the case in Ireland. There is extant a Book of Canons, attributed to Saint Patrick, but which bears internal evidence of belonging to the eighth century, one of which ordains that when the wife of a clergyman goes abroad she must wear a veil on her head. The learned Cardinal Moran enters into an elaborate argument to show that the canon does not imply a married clergy—that the wife referred to is after all not the clergyman's wife. The subject, however, is not one for argument, but for taking words in their plain and obvious meaning. I therefore give the canon in the original Latin, leaving it to the reader to translate, and to decide whether the deduction I have drawn from it is justified. It is as follows: 'Quicunque clericus ab hostiario usque ad sacerdotem sine tunica visus fuerit, atque turpitudinem ventris et nuditatem non tegat, et si non more Romano capilli ejus tonsi sint, et uxor [ejus] si non velato capite ambulaverit, pariter a laicis contemnentur, et ab Ecclesia separentur.'[1]

Shortly before the Anglo-Norman invasion, there is reason to believe that some of the highest ecclesiastical dignitaries in the land were married men; but, on the other hand, these cases must have been exceptional, for Giraldus Cambrensis, who delights in mentioning anything he can find disparaging to the Irish Church, whilst he charges the Irish clergy with habitual drunkenness, says that they are especially eminent for the virtue of continence, and goes on to remark that it may be considered almost a miracle that where wine has the dominion lust does not rule also. On the other hand, there was still in his day much resemblance between the Welsh and the Irish; and he tells us that in the Welsh Church there was to be found a married clergy, for he says, 'The sons after the decease of their fathers succeed to the ecclesiastical benefices not by election, but by hereditary right, possessing and polluting the sanctuary of God.' He also tells us that the same habit was followed in Brittany—a

---

[1] Haddan and Stubbs *Councils and Eccl. Documents relating to Great Britain and Ireland*, vol. ii. p. 328. Some MSS. omit the word *ejus*, put in brackets above, and the cardinal builds greatly on this. To any ordinary person, 'a man and wife' and 'a man and *his* wife' would mean the same thing.

place where Celtic influence continued until a very late date. The married clergy of Wales were an old institution, for we have the curious record under the year 961 : 'The same year Padarn, Bishop of Llandaff, died, and Rhodri, son of Morgan the Great, was placed in his room, against the will of the Pope, on which account he was poisoned. And the priests were enjoined not to marry without the leave of the Pope, on which account a great disturbance took place in the diocese of Tielaw, so that it was considered best to allow matrimony to the priests.'[1]

In the case of the Irish abbots it, no doubt, must often have happened that the tribal instincts would prove stronger than the ecclesiastical, and that a married abbot would be chosen in preference to one of another family. The general tendency, however, seems to have been towards celibacy, but without imposing it as a hard and fast rule.

As to the difference between the Irish and Romish doctrine of confession and absolution, nothing need be added to what has been already said in connection with the 'soul friend.'

There were also some differences of ritual. The Irish Church had its own peculiar liturgy until the time of the Anglo-Normans. They administered baptism with rites different from those of Rome, using single instead of trine immersion, and omitting the use of chrism. But it is not necessary that we should go into these minor details—all the more so as our sources of information are very scanty.

The points of difference between the Church of Ireland (or, to speak more correctly, the Celtic

---

[1] Haddan and Stubbs.

Churches, for the Scotch, British, and in many respects the Armorican Churches agreed with it) and the Churches of Western Europe may therefore be classed under seven heads:—

1. Independence of Rome.
2. Method of computing Easter.
3. Tonsure.
4. Ordinal.
5. Toleration of Married Clergy.
6. Public instead of Auricular Confession.
7. Ritual and Liturgy.

CHAPTER XII.

CONCLUSION OF THE EASTER CONTROVERSY.

For a considerable time the two Churches with their diverse usages existed side by side in England, not without considerable friction. Matters were at length brought to a crisis by the inconvenience of having two Easters in the house of Oswy, King of Northumberland. The monarch himself followed the Irish computation, as did most of the clergy in his kingdom. The queen had been educated by the Roman missionaries, and followed the rule that was propounded by them. The result was that while one part of the household was keeping the fast of Lent, another part was celebrating the feast of Easter. It was then proposed to get over the difficulty by having a public discussion of the question in the presence of the king, and whichever side brought forth the best arguments was to be followed by the whole kingdom.

It is remarkable that when the matter came thus to be argued, the speakers on both sides were from Irish monasteries. On the Romish side was Wilfrid, who had received his early education at Lindisfarne. After leaving that place he had travelled much, both in France and Italy, had been treated with great honour by the ecclesiastics of both countries, and had returned to England full of admiration for Romish ceremonies and altogether in sympathy with Romish ideas. The first ecclesiastical office which he held in England was that of abbot of a monastery from which the Irish had been ejected, because they, 'being left to their choice, would rather quit the place than adopt the Catholic Easter and other canonical rites according to the custom of the Roman Apostolic Church.' His opponent in the controversy was Colman, Bishop of Lindisfarne, who had been sent out from Iona.

The result of the discussion was a foregone conclusion. When the Irish had already been made to choose between conformity to Rome and expulsion from the king's dominions, it was not hard to guess to which side that king's verdict would be most favourable. He decided against the Irish use. Most of the Saxons who had been instructed in the Irish way were contented to abide by the king's decision. But Colman, with many followers, both English and Irish, chose to retire rather than conform. 'Perceiving that his doctrine was rejected and his sect despised,' he returned to Iona, and afterwards settled with his followers at Innisboffin, 'the island of the white heifer,' off the west coast of Ireland.

Meanwhile, an effort, though not a very vigorous one, was made to bring the Irish Church itself to the Roman way of thinking. Laurentius, who was successor of Augustine in the see of Canterbury, wrote a letter in the year 605 to the 'Lords, bishops and abbots throughout all Ireland.' Only the beginning of this epistle has been preserved. And it seems to have been altogether without effect, as indeed might have been expected. It was not by such easy-going efforts that the Irish would be induced to give up the usages to which they had been for so long a time accustomed.

In 634 Pope Honorius addressed a letter to the

Irish, 'earnestly exhorting them not to think their small number, placed in the utmost borders of the earth, wiser than all the ancient and modern Churches of Christ throughout the world'; and a further letter from Pope John IV. was sent shortly afterwards, in response to a letter of inquiry from some of the bishops of Ireland. In all these the keeping of Easter was the principal—one might almost say the only—subject discussed.

The point was eventually settled by the Irish themselves. The contests between their missionaries and the Romans, both in England and on the Continent, and the travels undertaken by some of their most eminent men, made them aware that their practice in this respect was singular, and naturally led them to study the subject on their own account. The south of Ireland, where there was most of this foreign intercourse, was the first to conform to the Roman method of computation.

The chief mover in bringing about the change was Cummian, who had formerly belonged to Iona, but who afterwards joined the Romish party. He wrote an apologetic letter on the subject, which is still preserved, and which is a remarkable production in its way. It displays very considerable learning, and it tells us that, however much the doctrines of the ancient Irish differed from those of Irish Protestants of to-day, the spirit displayed then was very much the same as now. The fact that any practice was followed by the Church of Rome was enough to condemn it in their eyes, however innocent it may have been in itself. He represents the upholders of the Irish custom as saying, 'Rome errs, Jerusalem errs, Alexandria errs, the whole world errs; the Irish and the Britons alone think right.' His plea is one for mere toleration; and his words on this subject would be worthy of remembrance in more modern controversies: 'What I am saying is, I perceive, a burden to you; what you say is also a burden to me, unless you shall prove it by the word of Holy Scripture. Let us then bear one another's burdens, and so shall we fulfil the law of Christ. For if we wound each other's weak conscience, it is against Christ we sin.'

The conciliatory spirit displayed, and the excellence of the arguments brought forward, had their desired effect. The early years of the seventh century saw the whole of Munster following the Roman computation. It was not, however, until a century later that the north of Ireland and Iona followed, and that conformity was established all through the land. But as this result was brought about by the arguments and investigations of members of the Irish Church itself, the alteration was made without any surrender of independence. The change, too, was a gradual one; and while it removed one of the barriers which prevented the Church of Ireland and the Church of Rome from coalescing, and thus prepared the way for events that happened some centuries later, it is to be remembered that these further changes were as yet in the distant future. On the one hand, no serious effort was made on the part of Rome to bring the Irish Church into subjection; and on the other hand, the Irish Church, in admitting greater friendliness than before, had no intention of bartering her liberties, or of occupying any other than the independent position which she had held from the first.

CHAPTER XIII.

THE EIGHTH CENTURY.

SEVERAL writers have remarked that the eighth century is a barren one in Irish ecclesiastical history. The Easter controversies were brought to a conclusion in its early years, and the Danish invasions belong to the next century. No great event happened in the meantime. It is therefore in one sense a period that has no history.

Even in political affairs the time was comparatively uneventful. A great battle was fought at the beginning of the century between the hereditary enemies, Meath and Leinster, in which the latter were victorious. In another great battle the Meath men avenged their defeat. Otherwise the period has little to record.

The quietude of the country caused the Church to increase in power and usefulness. The great schools of Ireland rose to the zenith of their glory. Many countries sent their sons to obtain education in the peaceful establishments of the Western Isle; and on the other hand, some of the alumni of the Irish schools, having left their native land, were distinguished for their brilliancy and learning in many a foreign kingdom. Such names as Clement and Albin, the wisdom-seekers, and Virgil the Geometer, are perhaps now seldom mentioned; yet in their day their fame had spread through many countries of Europe. Of the two first we have an interesting story given in the history of the times of Charlemagne. 'Two Scots of Ireland came to the shores of France with some British merchants. They were men who both in secular and sacred writings were incomparably learned. They used to expose nothing for sale, but to cry to the crowd who flocked round for the purpose of buying, If any of you wishes for wisdom, let him come to us and obtain it, for that is what we have on sale.'[1] Of the last, Virgil, who became Bishop of Salsburg, it is said that he anticipated the discoveries of later astronomers, and hardly escaped being condemned as a heretic for maintaining the existence of antipodes.

It is to this century that most of the illuminated manuscripts which still exist are to be attributed. In no age of the Church was the scribe held in such high esteem. 'Sixty-one remarkable scribes are named in the *Annals of the Four Masters* as having flourished in Ireland before the year 900, forty of whom lived between A.D. 700 and 800.'[2] If no other evidence were left to us than the books themselves, we should have reasons enough to conclude that the eighth century was an age of learning and art. Our only regret is that the remains of that period are so few. The Norseman of the next century cared little for books, and delighted in 'drowning' the volumes which came into his sacrilegious hands. Most of the precious manuscripts therefore have been destroyed, yet enough is left to make us pause in astonishment, for no other country has ever had scribes like these.

Connected with these manuscripts a very inter-

---

[1] Migne, *Patrol. Curs.*, tom. xcviii. p. 1371.
[2] Miss Stokes, *Early Christian Art in Ireland*, p. 10.

esting question arises. It is as to whether there existed a translation of the Bible peculiar to the Irish or Celtic Church. All the Irish Biblical manuscripts of the eighth century are, it is true, copies of the Vulgate; yet in many places they have readings peculiar to themselves. The subject is still one that awaits fuller investigation. Up to the present the Irish manuscripts have been regarded as the special possession of the archæologists. The Biblical critics do not seem to have thought of taking them in hand and collating them with other manuscripts of the same age. Their importance in this respect has, however, been partly realized, and Dr. Westcott says concerning them, that 'they stand out as a remarkable monument of the independence, the antiquity and the influence of British (Irish) Christianity.'[1]

Haddan and Stubbs have collected for us a large amount of evidence bearing on this point. They have taken the different quotations from Scripture to be found in the earliest Latin works written by Celtic authors; and they have compared them one with another, as well as with the Vulgate and with the old Latin translations which were in use in Africa and Italy before the time of Jerome. The conclusion they arrive at is that Saint Patrick was not acquainted with Jerome's Vulgate, but that after his time it gradually made its way in the Celtic Churches—traces of the old Latin being found as late as the tenth century. They say also that the evidence is 'exceedingly strong,' that the version thus gradually superseded was a special British and Irish revision of the old Latin.[2]

[1] Smith's *Dictionary of the Bible*, Art. 'Vulgate.'
[2] Haddan and Stubbs, *Councils and Ecclesiastical Documents relating to Great Britain and Ireland.*

It has been generally assumed that the Irish Church had no translation of the Bible into the vernacular. Haddan and Stubbs say briefly, 'There is no trace of any Celtic version of the Bible.' This is a mistake. There is actually in existence a copy of such a version, contained in an old manuscript volume, known as the *Speckled Book*, at present preserved in the library of the Royal Irish Academy. O'Curry tells as that this *Speckled Book* 'appears to have been written by some member of the learned family of the Mac Ægans, about the close of the fourteenth century. It is not a transcript of any one book, but, as will be seen, a compilation from various ancient books, preserved chiefly in the churches and monasteries of Connaught, Munster and Leinster.' Amongst its contents are found 'a Scripture narrative from the Creation to Solomon; the birth, life, passion and resurrection of our Lord.'[1] In another work[2] he speaks of this part as a 'translation, or rather paraphrase of the Old Testament,' and he gives two examples. One of these he renders into English in the very words of the Douay version of Exodus xv. 20; and the other, which is taken from 1 Samuel xxv. 18, he translates, 'The woman gave him five sheep, and two hundred loaves, and two *paits* (leather bottles) of wine'—a rendering which represents in a fairly accurate way the original Hebrew. If these are to be taken as examples of the work, there can be no doubt that there was in early times a translation of the Bible into Irish; and in any case the book gives evidence that the facts of Scripture were presented to the people in the language that they understood.

---

[1] O'Curry, *MS. Materials of Anc. Irish Hist.*, p. 352.
[2] *Manners and Customs of the Anc. Irish.*

It was the glory of the ancient Irish Church that she always prized the Word of God and taught it to her people. In this connection we cannot do better than quote from an old Irish treatise, said to have been written towards the close of the period we are now considering. 'One of the noble gifts of the Holy Spirit is the Holy Scripture, by which all ignorance is enlightened and all worldly affliction comforted; by which all spiritual light is kindled, by which all weakness is made strong. For it is through the Holy Scripture that heresy and schism are banished from the Church, and all contentions and divisions reconciled. It is in it well tried counsel and appropriate instruction will be found for every degree in the Church. It is through it the snares of demons and vices are banished from every faithful member in the Church. For the Divine Scripture is the mother and the benign nurse of all the faithful who meditate and contemplate it, and who are nurtured by it, until they are chosen children of God by its advice.' [1]

Although the eighth century was in one sense uneventful, we are not to suppose that it was without its important changes. Foremost among them was the bringing of Armagh into prominence, and the decline of the influence of Iona and the Columban monasteries. Up to the present, when we have spoken of Church life, of missionary labour, of religious controversy, it has been mostly in connection with Iona and its dependent establishments. Armagh has not played the same important part.

---

[1] From an Ancient Treatise on the Mass, contained in the *Speckled Book*. O'Curry, *MS. Materials*, p. 376. In the remainder of the extract given by O'Curry, the doctrine of the Real Presence is asserted, but not that of Transubstantiation.

All this was reversed by the time that the eighth century had drawn to a close. The Four Masters refer to Armagh only six times in their annals of the seventh century. In the eighth century they have twenty-three references, and in the ninth fifty-one. On the other hand, Iona, which is referred to twenty times in the eighth century, is only mentioned seven times in the ninth. Let us inquire how these changes were brought about.

When Iona was first established, the south-west portion of Scotland was under the same government and bore the same name as the north-east of Ireland. Under the influence of Columba the Scotch portion became an independent kingdom. The immediate results of this change were small. The Scotch residents did not give up their nationality, but continued to interest themselves in the affairs of Ireland, and to take part in the tribal quarrels as before. Nevertheless, the ultimate result was inevitable. They were drawn towards the Picts, who were their near neighbours, and who, by the efforts of Columba and his followers, were gathered into the Christian Church, while they were separated by the sea from their own fellow tribes in Ireland. The Irish never regarded them as other than an outlying and uninfluential kingdom. In Scotland they soon became the most powerful of all the clans.

Iona and its daughter monasteries in Ireland, though thus disunited politically, were kept in close union by the power of missionary zeal. Men from different parts of the country—from Durrow and Swords and Derry and elsewhere—were coming and going to Iona, and passed through on their way to their work amongst the heathen—first the Picts and then the Saxons. Iona thus formed an outlet for enterprise and energy. The men of greatest learning and of greatest talent alike looked to her to provide scope for the employment of their abilities. All this was changed by the issue of the Easter controversies. The Saxons in a body went over to the Roman party, and those who refused to conform had to leave the country. The Irish missionaries were therefore compelled to retire from the field, and find for themselves other habitations. Thus Colman, as we have seen, led his small body of followers first to Iona, and then to the west coast of Ireland. There could scarcely have been a greater change, and we find it hard to understand how men who had been accustomed to the one life could ever have been able to endure the other. At Lindisfarne they directed a great spiritual enterprise. They were the religious leaders and teachers of the people. The work of education, of evangelization, and of the Christian ministry occupied their time; and they had besides the excitement of controversy, which though no doubt in many ways an evil, yet produces a certain amount of enthusiasm, and stimulates mental and spiritual activity in no inconsiderable degree. At Innisboffin all was changed. The missionaries were forced to become hermits. Every condition of existence was reversed. We are not surprised that some of them found the new *régime* unendurable, and that those who could work together with loyalty and good-will could not live together in comparative idleness, but had to separate into two distinct communities.

In Iona itself the change must have been very great. From the time of its foundation the very reason of its existence was its missionary work, and when suddenly its whole mission field was closed against it, the inmates must have felt that nothing short of a revolution had taken place. The preparation and training of workers—the consecration of missionary bishops and abbots—the solemn sending forth of labourers with the blessing of the community—the meetings at which reports of success and failure were discussed—all these, which formed the life and soul of the community, were at an end.

In Ireland, the Easter disputes divided the Church into two parties. Bede tells us of Adamnan, who had been abbot of Iona, and whose life of Saint Columba is one of our contemporary sources of information about this period. In the year 683 the Saxons made a descent upon Ireland, devastated the great plains of Meath, and returned to England bearing with them a multitude of captives and great spoil. The year following, Adamnan went into Saxonland to plead the cause of the prisoners, and conducted their case with so much skill that he obtained the release of those who had been carried away, and a 'full restoration of everything he asked.' During his stay amongst the English, he learnt much about the 'canonical rites of the Church,' which he seems never to have known before, and after a time 'changed his mind, and readily preferred those things which he had seen and heard in the English Church to the customs which he and his people had hitherto followed.'[1] Returning to Iona, he thought he could easily persuade his own people to follow his example. In this he was mistaken. So much did they resent his unfaithfulness to their traditional usages, that he soon found his position untenable, and he was forced to resign the abbacy and depart from them into Ireland. Here he met with greater success, and induced nearly the whole country, with the

---

[1] Bede, *Eccl. Hist.*, v. 15.

exception of those who belonged to the Columban monasteries, to accept the new ideas. There were therefore, as I have said, two parties: the followers of Columba on the one side, and the rest of the Irish Church on the other.

A little before this time, and probably in connection with these very Easter disputes, the King of Ireland had decreed that the monasteries of Columba should not enjoy the same privileges as those of Patrick, Finnian and Keiran; that is, that Iona and its dependencies should not be in as favourable a position with regard to immunity from taxation, and probably in other ways, as were the monasteries at Armagh, Clonard and Clonmacnois. Adamnan is said to have cursed the monarch for making this unrighteous law, but his own subsequent conduct only helped in the degradation of his order.

Armagh soon identified itself with the new doctrines, and as it was at this time rising into eminence, and was beginning to assert that supremacy which it afterwards obtained, its influence helped in great measure to destroy the old Irish peculiarities.

The documents belonging to this age have many of them been framed manifestly with a view to uphold the claims of Armagh. For example, the old manuscript volume known as the *Book of Armagh*, contains among other documents, a canon which provides that cases of extreme difficulty which are beyond the powers of ordinary judges are to be referred to 'the archbishop of the Irish, that is, of Patrick, and the examination of this abbot,' and if found too difficult for him, to 'the chair of the Apostle Peter, having the authority of the city of Rome.' This canon is said to have been decreed by Auxilius, Patrick, Secundinus and Benignus; but it need hardly be remarked that if really made by them and recognised by succeeding generations, much of the history which we have already sketched would have been impossible. It is generally believed to belong to the eighth century.

The biographies of Saint Patrick have all the same tendency. Incidents the most improbable were invented, and stories of miracles were told—all with the purpose of exalting Patrick, and making it appear that Armagh was the central point from which his work was directed. It is a remarkable fact, when taken in connection with the extraordinary number of Lives of Saint Patrick written from the eighth century onward, that Adamnan, the biographer of Columba, never mentions him; nor does Bede, whose information was derived from Columban sources, seem to have been aware of his existence. The first knowledge we have of him from any source besides his own works, is the simple phrase, 'Patrick our Pope,' used by Cummian in 634.

The influence of Armagh was for the most part directed to the bringing of Ireland into conformity with the practices of the Romans. The see rose into prominence as the upholder of the new fashions, and it was no doubt in turn helped in its struggle for supremacy by the exterior support which it thus obtained. The very name Celepedair, 'Servant of Peter,' borne by an abbot of Armagh who died in 757, tells us how this devotion to Rome was beginning to take root. Irish ecclesiastics were fond of taking names of this kind. For example, we have Maelpaudhrig, which means Servant of Patrick; Malcolm, Servant of Columba; Celetighearnach, Servant of Tighernach, and many others; but the saints they chose to serve were almost invariably natives of Ireland.

It ought perhaps also to be mentioned among the causes which led to the advancement of Armagh, that for thirty years of the eighth century the monastery numbered amongst its inmates Flaherty, King of Ireland, who, after a reign of seven years, relinquished his crown and took upon him the habit of a monk. The loyalty of the people would not be denied to the king because he no longer held the reins of government; nor did it follow that he had given up all ambition because he had ceased to be a monarch and had become an ecclesiastic.

But though the eighth century saw the preeminence of Armagh fairly established, we are not to suppose that this meant anything like the 'primacy' of modern times. Ireland had many who were called archbishops from the very first, but they were merely men eminent among their own order. 'Arch' was nothing more than a prefix of excellence, and might be applied to any office in the Church, and so we have arch-lector, arch-senior, arch-soul-friend, and the like. That some at this time entertained the idea of establishing a real arch-bishopric at Armagh is more than probable, and no doubt this would have been accompanied by a submission of the Church of Ireland to the see of Rome. Both these projects were postponed for some centuries by the events that were about to happen. It was not until the year 1152 that metropolitans were appointed in Ireland. Four of the Irish bishops were then raised to the rank of archbishop by the Pope, and received the pall at the hands of his legate.

CHAPTER XIV.

THE DANISH INVASIONS.

THE position of Ireland, at the extreme west of Europe, has rendered it less liable to invasion than countries otherwise more advantageously situated. England was conquered by Romans and Saxons; but the former never set foot on Irish soil, and the latter only came on insignificant plundering expeditions. The third invasion of England, however, was one in which Ireland had its share. In the year 787, three ships of Northmen from Denmark appeared off the south coast of England. Eight years later they had made their way round to the coast of Antrim.

The story of their invasions is in many respects very similar for both countries. First, they came only in small parties, as pirates rather than invaders, their one object being plunder. Then they formed larger and better organized expeditions; they boldly attacked strongholds and fortresses; assumed the offensive in warfare, and endeavoured to dethrone the reigning sovereigns and usurp their authority. Finally, they made for themselves settlements, built cities, and erected castles, relinquishing more or less their roving and unsettled life, and making for themselves a home in the land which they had gained with their swords.

We should, however, be quite mistaken in supposing that the Danes of Ireland ever came in such formidable numbers as those who landed on the coast of England, or that the struggle with the invaders ever reached such a pitch of intensity as when in England the Saxons had to fight for their very national existence. Only once was there anything even remotely approaching an attempt to subjugate the whole island. On that occasion, a Norse leader named Turgesius is said to have united the different bands which up to that time had acted independently. With their help he made an attack simultaneously on different parts of the country, defeated the native kings, and set himself up as chief monarch of the land. The story is one highly coloured, and abounding in dramatic incidents. The subjugation of the country is said to have been so complete that all the churches were destroyed, all schools closed, all meetings prohibited. Every village had a Danish ruler. Every house had in it a Danish soldier. Every adult had to pay a tribute to the Danes for the mere right to live. The tyranny lasted for thirty years, until at length the country was delivered by the valour of fifteen beardless youths, who, disguised as maidens, went as escort to the king's daughter, after a demand had been made by Turgesius that she should be delivered up to him. These, suddenly producing daggers from beneath their robes, killed the principal Danish warriors, made the Viking leader himself a prisoner, and then raised the cry of battle from one end of the land to the other.

That this whole story is founded on fact is no doubt true; but it seems equally certain that it has been greatly exaggerated. The works of the Norse chroniclers are searched in vain for any mention of Turgesius, and this omission effectually disposes of the idea that he was such a great leader as he is generally represented to be. On the other hand, the *Annals of the Four Masters*, which are very full in their record of the Danish incursions, only mention his name once, and the events which they narrate for the years in which he is said to have held sway would have been quite impossible if a tithe of the story of his oppression were true. The principal source of our information respecting him comes from English authors, like Giraldus Cambrensis, who imagined that the number and fierceness of the Danish warriors in England was to be taken as the measure of their strength in Ireland; and who, when they met with a good story, had not the remotest idea that it was the duty of a historian to reject it, merely because it was not true.

On this whole subject of the Danish invasions there has been an immense amount of exaggeration. On the one hand, their insignificant piratical expeditions have been spoken of as if they were great national movements; and on the other, they have been credited with the introduction of that art and civilization which they did their best to destroy. There is perhaps no better corrective to the extraordinary statements which have been made on this subject than the study of local names. Nearly fourteen hundred names of Danish origin have been enumerated in the middle and northern counties of England. This tells us that there was a real invasion, carried on by an overwhelming and victorious force. Not more than fifteen of such names can be found in the whole of Ireland, and these are nearly all on the east coast.[1] We may therefore conclude that nothing more than small seaport settle-

---

[1] See Joyce, *Irish Names of Places*, vol. i. p. 105.

ments were ever attempted, or at all events accomplished, by the Danes in Ireland.

When they first came, the religious establishments, especially those on the coasts and in the islands, were the greatest sufferers. The Norsemen have obtained for themselves a historical reputation for bravery. It is doubtful if this reputation would ever have been gained if they had nothing to show but the record of their campaigns in Ireland. Their first attacks were all directed against the monasteries. In them they encountered the least resistance, for though ecclesiastics sometimes joined in battle, they were necessarily for the most part given to peace. The monasteries, too, had the greatest wealth, and that of a portable kind. In them were produced the works of gold and silver and metal—in them the stores of industry were garnered—in them were to be found costly shrines, book covers and altar vessels, curiously wrought and adorned with precious stones. In them, therefore, were the greatest hopes of plunder. As soon as the work of pillaging was accomplished, they retreated to their ships. They risked as few combats as possible. Once on board their vessels, they knew that they were safe.

In the year 795 they made their first appearance, when a small company landed on the island of Rathlin, off the coast of Antrim, burnt the houses and churches, and carried off the shrines and all the other valuables they could find. Three years later they attacked the little island of Innispatrick, opposite Skerries. There the remains of Saint Dochonna were preserved in a shrine, which the Norsemen broke and carried away. Then, sailing towards the north, they cruised along the coast, landing and plundering whenever they found a favourable opportunity.

Iona, from its exposed situation, suffered more than any other place. In 802 the Norsemen landed and burned a great part of the establishment. In 806 they returned with a larger force, and seemed determined to destroy it completely. Everything on which they could lay their hands was seized; sixty-eight of the inmates were killed, and the rest, hastily embarking in their coracles, and bringing with them whatever valuables they could collect, escaped to Ireland, made their way to the monastery of the same order at Kells, and there built a church and erected 'as it were a new Iona.'

As the years went by they arrived in greater numbers. They even ventured inland, and met the native Irish in pitched battles. But till stheir tactics were the same. Churches and monasteries were the prey for which they sought, until in the end there was not a religious establishment of importance in Ireland which had not suffered more or less at their hands.

It is not an unnatural mistake that many historians, both ancient and modern, have made in supposing that these expeditions of the Danes had a religious character, and that their deliberate aim was to destroy the Christian faith, and set up in its stead the worship of the Scandinavian deities. Among the stories about Turgesius is one, that at Armagh and Clonmacnois he actually used the Christian churches for the celebration of heathen rites, and that in the latter place his wife officiated as priestess. That such ideas should have been entertained at the time and have passed at once into history is not a subject of wonder; and yet any one who considers the question will see that this view of the case is most improbable, particularly when another and much simpler explanation is forth-

K

coming. The Norsemen were simply plunderers, and not religious enthusiasts; and they attacked the monasteries and churches, not because they hated Christianity, but because they found in them the most booty and the least resistance.

The result was almost as disastrous to the Irish Church as if the Danes had come of set purpose to destroy it. Amid all the troubles and disturbances of tribal warfare, the Irish had for the most part respected those peaceful settlements in their midst where the worship of God was celebrated. Occasionally, an act of sacrilege would be committed, but it was viewed with abhorrence by the nation in general. The result was that learning flourished, and the Church became more and more a power in the land. But the Danes changed all this. Bishops and teachers had to fly for their lives. Scribes saw their precious manuscripts in the rough hands of the barbarians, who took a brutal delight in destroying them, because they knew them to be so highly prized. And the native Irish were not long in following the pernicious example. Soon it came to be a recognised method of warfare that one chief should destroy the sanctuaries in the territory of his rival. Sometimes the churches of a whole province were ravaged because an unfriendly king was making war on its ruler. Under such circumstances learning could make but little progress. The Church itself became infected with the spirit of the age. The era of the 'saints and doctors' was at an end.

One of the more immediate results was the emigration of several Irish ecclesiastics to England and the Continent; and we learn incidentally that in the ninth century, as in the seventh, those churches which were in communion with the see of Rome refused to acknowledge the validity of the Irish ordinations. In a synod held at Chalons-sur-Saone in 813, one of the canons has the title 'On the nullity of the ordinations conferred by the Irish, who call themselves bishops.' And in 816, at a synod held at Cealcythe, in England, it was enacted that no one of the Irish race should be allowed to exercise any priestly function, the reason given being that amongst them 'neither rank is given to metropolitans nor honour to other bishops.'[1] This shows us that however much the Irish Church may have approximated to Romish doctrine, it had not gone far enough to be acknowledged as belonging to the Communion of the Romish Church.

[1] Both canons are given in Todd's *Life of St. Patrick* pp. 40, 43.

CHAPTER XV.

INFLUENCE OF THE DANISH INVASIONS ON THE CHURCH.

WE have seen that in the eighth century there was a decrease of influence in the Columban order, and a corresponding increase in the power of Armagh. The ninth century and the Danish invasions did still more for the diminution of the one and the advancement of the other. The repeated attacks made on Iona itself, and the transference from thence of the leading members of the community with all their most precious possessions was in itself a terrible blow. Kells, the 'new Iona,' never obtained the prestige of the old, and ceased after a time to be considered the mother church of the order. Derry afterwards obtained the pre-eminence: but this shifting of the central authority, accompanied as it was with frequent attacks from the barbarians, could only weaken the influence of the order, and quickly bring to an end that supremacy which it once enjoyed.

A serious dispute arose about this time between the followers of Columba and one of the most powerful of the Irish kings of the ninth century. We are quite in the dark as to how the controversy arose, or what were the questions on either side. We only know that in 814 'the families of Columkill went to Tara and solemnly cursed and excommunicated the king.' There was a time when such a ceremony would probably have cost the monarch his throne.

Tara itself was deserted simply because an ecclesiastic had cursed it. But the 'families of Columkill' were now of little account. The king was unmoved by the curse; the other churches in Ireland did not recognize the excommunication, and the monarch died at length in the odour of sanctity. Such an incident must have done much to diminish the already lessened influence of the Columban order.

On the other hand, the progress of Armagh was no less marked. Its inland position saved it from the first onslaughts of the Danes. While other churches were being burned and plundered, it remained in peace; and when, at length, it began also to taste the horrors of war, the struggle had become a national one, the whole country had been already aroused, and Armagh came to be regarded as a centre of national life. In the early years of the ninth century she had a succession of ambitious and able prelates, whose aim was not merely to uphold her ancient prestige, but to extend her influence all over the land. In connection with these abbots we have to notice the curious fact that their right to the position was fiercely contested, and that for the first fifty years of the century there were opposing lines of ecclesiastical succession. With the meagre information that we have on the subject, it is not easy now to decide exactly why this contention arose and continued so long. It is not improbable, however, that the opposing abbots were the nominees of rival kings, and that the contention was as much political as religious.

In the year 783 the rule of Armagh was extended over part of Connaught. Up to that time it would appear that Armagh stood alone—an important place, it is true, but without daughter establishments like those which belonged to Iona. In this year, however,

Dubdaleithe went to Cruachain for 'the promulgation of Patrick's law,' in other words, to bring the establishment under the control of Armagh, and to impose on it the same rules. This Dubdaleithe was the first to raise a contest as to the abbacy. Faindealach was the rightful occupant, and the two were in contention, setting up rival claims, as long as they lived.

Connaught was again visited by the Abbot of Armagh in 810, and in 822 an emissary named Airtri, with the aid of the reigning kings, caused all Munster to be brought into subjection. After that, he completed the work begun in Connaught, 'promulgating the law of Patrick among its three divisions;' and finally he endeavoured to eject his superior, Eoghan, the Abbot of Armagh, and set himself in his place. In this last, however, he was unsuccessful. Eoghan was soul friend to Niall, one of the most powerful chieftains of Ulster, and utilizing the influence which he thus possessed, he sent to him this quatrain, threatening him with the ecclesiastical curse if he did not take up arms in his favour :

'Say to Niall that not lucky for him will be the curse
  of Eoghan, son of Anmchad.
He will not be in the kingdom in which he is, unless
  his soul friend be abbot.'

The result was that the chieftains made the cause of the contending abbots their own. A fiercely contested battle was fought, which lasted three days, with the result that Niall was victorious and Eoghan was retained in his abbacy. Some members of the community would have wished the dispute to have terminated otherwise. One of the seniors of Armagh has left the record of his dissatisfaction in these words :—

'Not well have we gained our goal,
Not well have we passed by Leire,
Not well have we taken Eoghan
In preference to any pilgrim in Ireland.'

Eoghan's rival died before him; but no sooner had he himself passed away than the dispute sprang up afresh. Dermot, one of the ambitious school, became abbot, and proceeded to Connaught with the law of Patrick, for the western province does not seem to have taken kindly to the rule of Armagh, and required several successive efforts to bring it into subjection. In 834, however, Forannan was put up in opposition to Dermot, and the two continued as rival abbots until the death of both in the same year, 851.

These episodes deserve particular attention, and throw a great deal of light on the subsequent history. We see that the position of Abbot of Armagh had become so important that for years members of the royal families contended for its possession. We see, too, its influence becoming more and more widely extended, until the ruler at Armagh becomes ruler throughout the whole of Munster and Connaught, as well as of course Ulster, the province in which it is itself situated. An extension of power like this would be sure to arouse still greater ambitions. The time when the Abbot of Armagh was to enjoy archiepiscopal rank was as yet far in the distance, but the seeds were already sown which were sure to spring up in due time. Meanwhile, we may see how its political influence had increased, from an event which happened in the year 889. Two chieftains had 'conflict and dissension' at Armagh, and were with difficulty separated by the abbot. One would think that there the matter would have ended. A good deed had been done, and virtue might well have been left to be its own reward. Not so, however.

Each of the contending parties had to pay for the abbot's peaceful interference, and were mulcted in the sum of thirty times seven cumhals (a cumhal was the value of three cows); he was also required to give hostages for his future good behaviour, and to give up four of his followers to be hanged. Thus it will be seen that the Abbot of Armagh had become like one of the ordinary chiefs. Like them, he demanded his 'eric' or fine, for the offence committed, with the alternative of war.

There are few countries in which the Church has not, at some time or other, gained abnormal secular power. This has never worked for good. The weapons of the Church's warfare are not carnal, and when she lays aside the armour that belongs to her, and assumes that of the world, she ceases to be of any power in the pulling down of the strongholds of Satan.

It will not surprise us now to learn that not only at Armagh, but in most parts of the country, the Church became thoroughly secularized. Forced as it was to take up arms in its own defence against the Norse invaders, those arms soon came to be used in internecine strife. Abbots and bishops who ought to have been foremost in promoting peace, became foremost in stirring up causes of civil war, and joined in the battles themselves, forgetful of their sacred profession. In Munster the office of spiritual and civil ruler became united in one, and the succession of bishop-kings founded a kingdom so powerful that eventually it became the greatest in the whole country. The case of one of these bishop-kings will best illustrate the entire secularization of the Church, and the low ebb of spiritual life to which she was brought by the influences then at work.

A certain Felim united in himself the offices of

King of Munster and Bishop of Cashel in the early parts of the ninth century. We first find him associated with Airtri, Bishop of Armagh, in bringing the churches of Munster under the 'law of Patrick.' From this we might conclude that he took a great interest in the spiritual welfare of his kingdom; but when we see his subsequent career, and find also that this Airtri was put up as bishop in opposition to the nominee of the northern kings, we cannot help suspecting that this religious zeal covered an ambitious design—possibly the hope that he would become *Ardrigh*, or chief king, by the help of the northern bishop—a dignity that was actually obtained by one of his successors, the famous Brian Boru. The next thing we read of Felim is his attacking the district near Clonmacnois. Shortly afterwards he burned the churches of the same place, and killed numbers of the 'family.' The same year he was at Durrow in the King's County, where a Columban monastery existed, and he was still at the same work of sacrilege and devastation. He made several plundering expeditions into Connaught. He took the oratory at Kildare in defiance of Forannan, Bishop of Armagh. Several times he made incursions into Meath, plundering and burning wherever he went. Then he led an army towards Wexford, but King Niall went against him, and defeated him. In the account of the battle we learn incidentally that this precious bishop—'the devout Felim,' a bard calls him—had actually taken his crozier with him into the battle. Finally, he went again to Clonmacnois, and plundered the sanctuary once more. This time he met a spiritual foe. An internal disease took him, and the aggrieved ecclesiastics at once asserted that Saint Keiran had appeared to him, and had given him a thrust of his crozier. He lingered in mortal sickness for nearly a year, and in the end died of the 'internal wound inflicted by the miracle of God and Keiran.' After all this terrible record, the Annalists do not hesitate to speak of him as 'anchorite and scribe, the best of the Irish in his time.' And one of the bards wrote concerning him :

'There never went on regal bier a corpse so noble ;
  A prince so generous under the King of Albain never shall
    be born.'

If in Felim we have the bishop-prince at his worst, in Cormac, one of his successors, we have the same character at its best. He was a warrior, but not a plunderer; he had all the ability of a statesman, and at the same time he was the liberal patron of art and literature. Though he never actually secured supremacy for himself, he made it an easy task for his successors to place Munster at the head of all the kingdoms of Ireland. Yet his greatness was altogether that of a soldier and king; and from the very excellence of his character we can see how incongruous was the combination of secular and spiritual rule in the one person. We may admire the brave king leading his followers to battle, and falling in the midst of the fighting men ; but when we find him described as 'a bishop, an anchorite, a scribe, and profoundly learned in the Irish tongue,' we cannot help thinking that his place should have been in the quiet cloister, rather than in the noisy battle-field.

The monastic system of the Irish Church, modified as it was by the tribal organization, had proved itself excellent in many ways. It had provided peaceful retreats where pursuits of learning and industry might be followed, even in the midst of turmoil and strife. It had proved itself effectual as a missionary organization; but it failed to stand the test of time, and it utterly broke down under the strain of foreign invasion. A Church differently organized might not have produced so many 'saints' and men of learning, but it would not have suffered such complete demoralization merely because some of its sanctuaries had been destroyed.

CHAPTER XVI.

CONVERSION OF THE DANES.

By the middle of the ninth century the Danes had established themselves permanently in settlements along the coast, and had founded the seaport towns of Dublin, Waterford and Limerick. From that time they maintained a continuous warfare with the natives, and had varying success. Sometimes they penetrated into the interior of the country, at other times they were driven from their own strongholds; but notwithstanding these vicissitudes, their position remained practically unchanged. They never extended their dominions beyond the few cities at first occupied, and from these positions the Irish were never able permanently to dislodge them. Before long they took their place to all intents and purposes as one of the tribes of Ireland. They formed treaties with the different kings, and fought side by side with the natives in the tribal disputes which form so large a part of the history of the country at that time. After defeat, they were quite ready to give hostages, pay tribute, and acknowledge the supremacy of the Irish kings; but they held their ground, and as soon as they felt strong enough, they renewed the contest, and shook off the yoke that had been placed on them. This state of things continued down to the time of the Anglo-Norman invasion.

The Norsemen who thus made a settlement in the

land were at the first all pagans, and as far as we can learn, there was no serious effort made on the part of the Irish for their conversion. It was through the influence of their own compatriots in England that they were at length brought to the knowledge of the truth.

The Danes who landed in England found no insurmountable obstacle to prevent their coalescing with the Angles. They were of the same race, and spoke alosmt the same language; they had the same forms of government, and very nearly the same code of laws. When at one time the Danes became rulers of the nation, the transference of power was scarcely perceived by the people in general—the same laws and usages continued in force; it caused no break in the national life. It was more like a mere change of dynasty than the subjugation of the country by a foreign power. The political result was that Danes and Saxons became in the end one homogeneous people. The religious result was that the paganism of the Danes imperceptibly faded away, and that by degrees they accepted the religion of Christ, which was established all around them.

During all this time the Danes of Ireland did not forget their kinsmen beyond the Channel. Though settled in Dublin, or Waterford, or Limerick, they were not Irish. Just as in an earlier age the inhabitants of the south-west of Scotland belonged to the Irish, and not to the Pictish people, so these Danes were really Englishmen living in Ireland. In times of defeat they sent to England for help; and when some of their warriors could be spared from the defence of their possessions, they went across the water and took their part in the contests with Saxons and Britons which were being continually carried on. When the Danes of England became

Christian, the conversion of their brethren in Ireland followed as a matter of course. The change was very gradual, and the Christianity which they at first professed was very little removed from the paganism which they abandoned. Eventually, however, idolatry became quite extinct amongst them; they founded churches more imposing in proportions than any others to be found in Ireland, and they established a ritual and liturgy similar to that which was followed at the time by the Churches of England. It is not easy to assign dates to these events, but speaking generally, we may say that the conversion of the Danes was being accomplished from the middle of the tenth to the middle of the eleventh century. Ireland was thus brought for a second time in contact with the Church of England.

We have seen how in England the missionaries from Iona were forced to retreat before the paramount influence of Rome, and how the English Church thus became subject to the Pope. It was easier, however, to banish the teachers and abolish the ceremonies of the Irish than to alter the tone which they had given to the Church. Of course this, too, would have been changed in time, if the advantage gained by the Romanists had been vigorously followed up; but the unsettled state of the country, consequent on the Danish invasions, cut off England to some extent from intercourse with the Continent; and the result was that the Anglo-Saxon Church drifted into a state of quasi-independence. In theory it acknowledged the Pope, and was in communion with the other Churches on the Continent, but practically it was independent. 'It was to an extraordinary degree a national church: national in its comprehensiveness, as well as in its exclusiveness. . . . The interference of foreign Churches was scarcely, if at all, felt. There was no Roman legation from the days of Theodore to those of Offa, and there are only scanty vestiges of such interference for the next three centuries; Dunstan boldly refused to obey a papal sentence. Until the eve of the Conquest, therefore, the development of the system was free and spontaneous, although its sphere was a small one.'[1]

This independence was far from being an unmixed blessing. The fighting bishop became as well known in England as he had been in Ireland. 'Two West-Saxon prelates fell in the battle of Charmouth in A.D. 835; and Bishop Ealhstan of Sherborne acted as Egbert's general in Lent in A.D. 825, and was one of the commanders who defeated the Danes on the Parret in A.D. 845.'[2] Despite the efforts of reformers such as Dunstan, the Church had become secularized, and sorely needed an infusion of new life. Such was its condition when both Church and State were revolutionized by the Norman conquest.

One of the first acts of William the Conqueror was to place men of his own nation in all the most important bishoprics. These foreign ecclesiastics—men of ability and energy—set themselves to reproduce in England the state of things to which they had been accustomed on the Continent. Thus, when the realm of England was brought under the sway of the Conqueror, the Church of England was brought under the sway of the Pope.

With the exception of Donat, first Bishop of Dublin, who was consecrated in 1038, all the Danish bishops of Ireland were appointed subsequently to the advent of William the Conqueror. They were there-

---

[1] Stubbs, *Constitutional Hist. of England*, 2nd ed., vol. i. p. 245.
[2] *Ib.*, vol. i. p. 237.

fore, to all intents and purposes, Romish bishops. They all of them went to Canterbury for consecration, and regarded themselves as suffragans of the Primate of England. Some historians have seen in this submission 'a wholesale betrayal of the liberties of the Irish Church.' This, however, is a mistake. That it paved the way for the subjection of the Irish Church is true enough; but there was no betrayal. The case was exactly analogous to the case of Gibraltar at present. The Bishop of Gibraltar is subject to the Archbishop of Canterbury, not because he wishes to bring the Spanish Church into subjection to the Anglican metropolitan, but simply because Gibraltar is English, and not Spanish. In the same way the Danish bishops of Dublin were subject to Canterbury, because Dublin was an English and not an Irish city.

In the pontificate of Alexander II. it was ordered that no bishop should exercise his functions until he had received the confirmation of the Holy See. Possibly it was in pursuance of this edict that Patrick, second Bishop of Dublin, proceeded to Rome, after he had been consecrated by Lanfranc, Archbishop of Canterbury. Hildebrand, the actual framer of the decree, was then the occupant of the papal chair; and as he was always watchful for opportunities of extending the sway of that 'city of God,' which it was the one object of his life to establish, we can well believe that he gave directions to the Danish bishop to use his influence for the bringing of the Irish Church into a state of canonical obedience. At the same time he himself wrote to Turlogh O'Brien, King of Ireland, telling him that the Holy Church is placed above all the kingdoms of the earth, the Lord having put into subjection unto her principalities and powers and all that seems possessed of grandeur and dignity in the world, and that the Universal Church owes to Peter and to his vicars a debt of obedience, as well as of reverence. He then exhorts that this debt of obedience should be discharged by the Irish, and that they should cherish and maintain the Catholic peace of the Church. A few years afterwards Gilbert, Danish Bishop of Limerick, was appointed Papal Legate—the first that Ireland had ever seen. Waterford, too, had its Danish bishop consecrated at Canterbury. Thus the Church of Rome obtained a footing in the country. We shall see that it was not long before the whole Irish Church was brought under its power.

CHAPTER XVII.

RISE AND PROGRESS OF THE ROMISH PARTY.

WE must now retrace our steps, and ask how the Irish Church itself fared in that age which saw the conversion of the Danes and the establishment of a branch of the English Church on Irish soil. We have seen how the old monastic system broke down, and ceased to be an effective power against the surrounding lawlessness. Some of its worst features, however, survived. From the first, the rule was followed that wherever possible the abbot of every monastery should be of the same family as the founder. This easily developed into a kind of heredity. Celibacy, though encouraged, was never very strictly enjoined, and often the abbacy or bishopric passed from father to son. When ecclesiastical positions became sources of wealth and influence, they were as jealously confined to the ruling families as were the offices of king and chieftain. In Armagh the one family kept possession of the see for two hundred years, and Bernard of Clairvaux stigmatizes it as 'an evil and adulterous generation, for although clergy of that race were sometimes not to be found amongst them, yet bishops they never were without.'[1]

It is, however, not at all certain that this condem-

---

[1] Bernard, *Life of Malachy.*

nation was fully deserved. The turning of the bishopric into a hereditary office was no doubt a great evil; still, it is well to remember that the authority of the hereditary abbot and bishop (for both offices were now united) was cheerfully recognized by bitterly opposing factions. The period of which we are treating saw a long-continued struggle between North and South; but the kings of Munster were as ready to acknowledge Armagh as were those of Ulster. Perhaps, after all, this very hereditary succession secured the peace of the Church as nothing else could have done. If reigning families fought for spiritual as they did for temporal power, the whole country would have relapsed into barbarism, and soon no religion of any kind would have been left.

I have shown that as Armagh increased in power there was a corresponding decrease in the influence of the Columban order. In the period we are now considering, Armagh occupies by far the most prominent part of the history. But it is to be remembered that the materials at our disposal for the history of this period are nearly all derived from sources in sympathy with Armagh, and that therefore it is hard for us to say in how far it really enjoyed ecclesiastical pre-eminence. When we read of a bishop resigning one see because he has been appointed to another, we naturally conclude that the new appointment is one of more importance than the old. This is what actually happened in 988. Dubhdalethe was Abbot and Bishop of Armagh. He was an able and ambitious man. He aspired to the abbacy before it was vacant; and Muiredeach, who held the see in 966, was set aside in his favour. In 973 he made a circuit of the churches of Munster, demanding and obtaining tribute from them. In 985 he asserted his rights against the monarch of Ireland. The king had removed the shrine of Saint Patrick from Ardee to Assey on the river Boyne. For this not very heinous offence he was obliged to pay a heavy fine to Dubhdalethe, giving tribute from every portion of his kingdom. Some of the bishop's historical poetry remains; he was therefore a bard as well as an ecclesiastic, and in that age this would have added greatly to his reputation.

In 988 he 'assumed the coarbship of Columkill by the advice of the men of Ireland and Alba.'[1] Ten years he continued in his new office, and in the meantime Muireagan of Bordoney took his place as Abbot of Armagh and Coarb of Saint Patrick. That a man such as Dubhdalethe appears to have been, would have relinquished a greater for a lesser position, is not to be believed. We are therefore led to conclude that as late as the end of the tenth century the Coarb of Columkill took rank above the Coarb of Patrick. We have no other example that we can place beside this, and the incident is therefore to be regarded as the last token of that ascendency which Iona had once enjoyed.

One hundred years later, the see of Armagh had advanced immensely. There could no longer be any question as to its supremacy. The abbot had become a veritable prince of the Church, imposing and receiving tribute from all parts of the country. But in other respects he had few of the prerogatives of an archbishop. It was by no means considered necessary that his advice should be asked or sanction obtained before other bishops were consecrated. They owed him no canonical obedience. They did not repair to him for ordination.

---

[1] *Annals of the Four Masters*, A.D. 988.

Under the old Irish monastic system, the bishop was merely one of the officers of the community. Nearly every monastery had a bishop—sometimes more than one—amongst its inmates. When that system broke down, the effect of this unusual arrangement remained. In some cases the bishops had for diocese the territory of the tribe to which they belonged—in other cases they seem to have had no jurisdiction. Anselm of Canterbury complains concerning them, 'The episcopal honour suffers no little disparagement when he who is invested with the pontificate knows not when he is ordained where he is to go, or over what certain place he is to preside in his episcopal ministry.' Every bishop felt quite free to consecrate another bishop, if he were a man of learning and eminence, even though he was to have no diocesan authority. The rule of requiring three consecrators was one that had never been followed in the Irish Church. It is manifest that all this would require to be completely changed before the head of Armagh could in any real sense be said to be an archbishop. At first the exaction of tribute was all that was desired; but afterwards foreign travel made the heads of the Church acquainted with the ecclesiastical arrangements of other countries; and nearer home, the three Danish bishops rendering canonical obedience to the Archbishop of Canterbury, furnished a pattern which the ambitious prelates of Armagh soon endeavoured to reproduce in Ireland.

The first steps towards thus modifying the constitution of the Church of Ireland were taken by Ceallach, who became Coarb of Patrick by the election of the men of Ireland in A.D. 1105. He was not forgetful of the temporalities of his see. In Ulster he exacted 'a cow from every six persons, or a heifer in calf for every three persons, besides many other offerings.' In Munster he obtained 'seven cows, seven sheep, and half an ounce of silver from every cantred, besides many jewels.' Other places gave him similar offerings. When the see of Dublin became vacant by the death of Bishop Samuel in 1121, Ceallach assumed the episcopal office in that city. Bishops were elected by the votes of both clergy and laity, and he obtained a majority in his favour. Although Dublin was a Danish kingdom, the Irish in it far outnumbered the Danes, and on an occasion like this could secure the election of any candidate they pleased. But the minority of foreigners were not to be baffled in this way. Seeing that they were outvoted at the first assembly, they held another meeting on their own account; selected one of themselves, Gregory, a layman, for the vacant post; sent him off to Canterbury for consecration to all three orders of the ministry, and wrote at the same time a letter to the archbishop, requesting him to promote their nominee to the order of episcopacy, if he wished to retain Dublin under his jurisdiction, or that otherwise the rights of Canterbury would be usurped by Armagh.

Ceallach was equally energetic in the reformation of what he considered to be defects in the government of the Church. He assembled synods at different places, and caused enactments to be made reducing the number of bishops, appointing to each bishop his diocese, and imposing on them, as far as possible, the obligation of canonical obedience to himself.

In these efforts he found an able helper, or rather director, in Gilbert, Danish Bishop of Limerick. This Gilbert had been the disciple of Anselm, had been accustomed in his early days to the ecclesiastical arrangements of France, was a devoted adherent of the Papacy, and was the first in Ireland who ever held the office of legate to the Pope. To his mind the irregularities of the Irish Church rendered it schismatical. He therefore spared no labour in endeavouring to bring the liturgy and government of the Church into conformity with England and Rome. He attended the synods which Ceallach assembled, and helped to frame their canons. According to Romish authorities, he presided at these synods in his capacity of papal legate. The Irish Annalists, however, say that it was Cellach who presided.

No immediate success crowned these labours. The institutions which had existed from the very first were not to be so easily set aside. It was not difficult to frame rules. It was a task of much greater magnitude to put the rules into practice. One thing was soon made evident: that no effectual change could be brought about so long as the hereditary system of succession to ecclesiastical appointments prevailed. Armagh itself was the greatest offender of all in this respect, and its wonderful growth in importance made it the subject of special notice. Cellach was a member of the family that for two hundred years had thus obtained possession of the see. It seemed therefore as if the greatest obstacle of all was without remedy.

On the death of Cellach, an effort was made to break through this long prescription. He was at Ardpatrick in the County Limerick at the time when he was taken with his last sickness, and had therefore near him Gilbert and those who were urging him on in his schemes of reformation. Under their influence he was induced on his death bed to make a kind of will, appointing Malachy, Bishop of Down and Connor, to succeed him in the see of Armagh. This would have been to introduce new blood into the succession, and by bringing in one whose sympathies were decidedly with the Romish movement to pave the way for still greater changes. That an episcopal see should be treated as a legacy and made the subject of a will was of course contrary to all order. It was just as uncanonical as the hereditary succession which it was intended to displace; but it seems to have been thought that in no other way could the old arrangement be broken through; and, as a matter of fact, it eventually accomplished all that was intended.

Not at first, however, nor in the way that had been anticipated. Cellach's successor was appointed from the same family, in utter disregard of any claims that Malachy could put forward. The new bishop, Murtagh, took possession of the insignia of office—the Book of Armagh, and the ancient crozier, known as the Staff of Jesus, and having these he was acknowledged by the whole country as the rightful coarb. Gilbert assembled a synod of clergy, in which the claims of Malachy were upheld. But the time had not yet come when the Pope's legate could assert his authority as such; so it was all to no purpose. Then, as now, possession was nine points of the law. Murtagh had possession of the see, and he retained it to the day of his death.

As soon as the bishopric was again vacant, the struggle was renewed. Niall, kinsman of the deceased prelate, was immediately installed in his place; but this time, partly by physical force and partly by purchase, Niall was deposed, and Malachy took his place. The next year, however, the contest was renewed; the abbacy was restored to Niall, and Malachy was again without his coveted prize.

After this Malachy gave up the contest, and devoted himself to the carrying out of his designs in a different way. He professed to be contented with his small diocese of Connor, but he managed that another rival should be put in opposition to Niall. Against himself there seemed to be a popular prejudice, and it suited him as well to have in Armagh one whom he could bend to his own will. A bishop, therefore, was brought from Derry, Melbride O'Brolcan, one of a family that had been for many years most influential in the Irish Church. He was put up in opposition to Niall, and receiving the popular suffrages was made coarb in his stead. From what we know of the O'Brolcans, it is very doubtful whether Melbride would have lent himself to the designs of Malachy; but the question never arose. Scarcely had he enjoyed his elevation for two years when he died. The same year Niall passed away, and thus at length every obstacle seemed to have been removed. Malachy, however, made no further attempt to assert his right; but he managed to secure the election of Gelasius, one like-minded with himself, who was contented to take him as guide and leader in everything.

Bishop Gelasius was appointed in the year 1139, and retained his bishopric until 1174. Between these two years lie some of the most eventful incidents of Irish history. He himself changed his position of simple Coarb of Patrick for the more magnificent rank of Archbishop of Armagh and Primate of all Ireland. When he was appointed, Ireland was a nation; when he died, it was an English province. A similar change passed over the Church. When he was appointed, the Church of Ireland was independent; when he died, it had been brought into subjection to the see of Rome.

Gelasius, however, was one who had greatness thrust upon him. In all these events he was a leading figure, yet his actions were for the most part controlled by others. The real work of subjecting the Church of Ireland to the see of Rome was done by Malachy.

With regard to this Malachy we have a very remarkable source of information. His Life has been written by no less a personage than Bernard of Clairvaux. From that life we learn that in his early years he came under the influence of the Danish Bishop of Waterford, that he learnt the Romish method of chanting and of saying the Mass, and became so much enamoured with foreign usages and ways, that in the end he became quite unlike an Irishman. 'He was born in Ireland,' says Bernard, 'of a barbarous race. There he was educated; there he received the knowledge of letters; but for the rest he drew no more from the barbarous country of his birth than the fishes of the sea draw from their native element.'

Bernard's life is a panegyric, and he intends these words for praise. They explain to us why his friends were among the Danish bishops rather than the Irish, why his sympathies were with Rome rather than with his own country, and why he preferred the gorgeous ritual of the continental churches to the simple modes of worship in his own.

Bernard, whose information must have been largely derived from Malachy himself, speaks of Irish Christianity as if it were no better than paganism. Thus he describes the diocese of Connor, telling us that when Malachy first went there, 'this man of God saw that he had to deal not with men, but with beasts. Nowhere had he met such people, no matter how barbarous the place; nowhere had he found any so froward in their manners, so gloomy in their forms of worship, so unfaithful to their oaths, barbarous in their laws, stiff-necked with regard to discipline, unclean in their lives; Christian in name; in reality, pagans.'

After this terrible tirade he descends to particulars, and it is quite a relief to find that the awful crimes which he so unsparingly condemns are as follows: 'They did not give either tithes or first-fruits; they did not enter into lawful wedlock; they did not make confessions; there could not be found any who either desired penance or would impose it.' This, after all, was only saying that the Church of Ireland was primitive, and not Roman. The only serious charge in the list—that they did not enter into lawful wedlock—can only mean that their marriage rites were not like those of the Romans, for we have abundant evidence that conjugal fidelity was at that time strictly enforced and observed.

In another place he tells us that 'there was throughout the whole of Ireland a relaxation of ecclesiastical discipline, a weakening of authority, a mere empty kind of religion. Everywhere instead of Christian gentleness there has crept in unaware a savage barbarism; indeed, it is a kind of paganism that has been introduced under the Christian name.' Here, again, is a very sweeping statement, and we might be led to conclude from it that religion had altogether departed from the island. We are reassured, however, when we read on, and find that what he means by 'savage barbarism' and 'paganism' is that 'bishops are changed and multiplied, without order, without reason, at the will of the metropolitan, so that one bishopric was not contented with one bishop, but that almost every church must have its own separate bishop.' This was no doubt contrary to ecclesiastical law, but it was the system in vogue when Ireland showed her religious vitality by her missions, and when the successful and enthusiastic preachers of her race contrasted most favourably with the faint-hearted workers sent from Rome.

Although, therefore, Bernard's work is useful and instructive, it must not be implicitly followed. Happily we have other and more reliable sources of information, which enable us to correct in some measure the extravagances into which he allowed himself to be led. One idea, however, runs through the whole of his book. It is that the Church of Ireland did not acknowledge the authority of the Pope, and was not in ecclesiastical subjection to him. The *Life of Malachy* is meaningless on any other assumption. The life-work of Malachy was to bring about a change in this respect. It is for this that he is lauded by his biographer. It was in recognition of his success that he obtained the unique honour of being the first Irishman resident in Ireland who was canonized by the Pope. If the Irish Church was already subject to Rome, the whole biography is inexplicable.

We have already noted the doctrines and usages in which the Church of Ireland differed from Rome in the seventh century. We are now at the twelfth. It may be well to pause again, and ask how the case stood after five hundred years had passed away.

The controversies as to the time of keeping Easter and of the mode of tonsure had become things of the past. In the other points which have been noted, the old customs survived, and the position of the Church was very much the same in the twelfth century as in the seventh. The attitude with regard to the Pope was unchanged. His supremacy was neither admitted nor rejected. It was simply ignored. This was shown very clearly in the way in which bishops and the more powerful ecclesiastics were appointed. Clergy and laity alike had their voice, and when their votes were given, no other sanction was thought necessary. When, as in the case of Malachy, a candidate came with the recommendation of the Papal legate, he was promptly rejected, and the popular nominee successfully held the place against him.

In the matter of ordinations exactly the same differences continued as before. Only one bishop officiated in the consecration of new bishops, and the institution of archbishop did not exist. The celibacy of the clergy was little insisted on, and in the higher orders was seldom followed. Auricular confession was unknown, as was priestly absolution and the so-called sacrament of penance. They still had their peculiar liturgy, stigmatized by the Pope's legate as schismatical, and so different from the Romish that a person accustomed to the one form of worship found himself unable to follow the service when the other form was employed. In baptism they still omitted the use of chrism.

That many believed in the doctrine of transubstantiation is more than probable. That the doctrine was not universally received is shown by an interesting incident related by Bernard. The case arose in Lismore. This was one of the places where an old Irish monastery existed, with an Irish monastic bishop and abbot. No sooner, however, was a Danish bishop appointed to the neighbouring town of Waterford than he began styling himself 'Bishop of Lismore,' as if he were the representative of the old Irish Church, whereas he really had no jurisdiction beyond the walls of the town, and was by education and ordination an Englishman. One of the Irish clergy in this place,—' a man of exemplary life, so it is said '—gave public expression to his views on the Holy Communion. 'He, being wise in his own eyes, presumed to say that in the Eucharist there was only a sacrament, and not the thing represented by the sacrament; that is to say, that there is only a consecration, and not the true Body.' Malachy reasoned with him in private, but it was all to no purpose. Then a meeting was summoned, from which, contrary to the Irish customs, the laity were excluded. Here ' he endeavoured with all the strength of no mean abilities to assert and defend his error.' Malachy met him first with argument and then with threatening, but all to no purpose. He left the meeting ' discomfited but not corrected,' and protesting that ' he was conquered not by reasoning, but overpowered by the authority of the bishop.' A sentence of excommunication was pronounced against him, but he was still unmoved. 'Thou, O Malachy,' he said, 'without reason thou hast condemned me this day. Thou hast spoken not only contrary to the truth, but against thine own conscience.' Then turning to the rest of the assembly he added, ' All you care for the man rather than the truth. I accept no man's person, if in doing so I must forsake the truth.'

Bernard tells us that this sturdy Protestant repented on his death bed ; but he never admits that Malachy made a mistake or failed in any enterprise he took in hand. He altogether suppresses the fact that Malachy was unable to retain the see of Armagh, and attributes to his great humility his retreat from the position which he found to be untenable. We may therefore be excused for suspecting that this incident of the death-bed repentance is an embellishment put in by Bernard to save the credit of his hero. But whether this be the case or not, the significance of the incident remains the same. The denial of the doctrine of transubstantiation comes from an Irish clergyman. The assertion of the doctrine and condemnation of the heretic comes not from the Irish, but from the Romish party. There can be no doubt, however, that the leaven of Romanism was spreading, and that the country was thus being prepared for the important events which were shortly to take place.

CHAPTER XVIII.

THE SYNOD OF KELLS.

WHEN Malachy had secured the election of Gelasius to Armagh, the way seemed clear for the carrying out his scheme for Romanizing the Church of Ireland. With this end in view, one of his first acts was to repair to Rome, and seek a personal audience with the Pope. On his way he visited the monastery at Clairvaux and made the acquaintance of Bernard, who afterwards became his biographer. When he arrived at Rome, he was graciously received by Pope Innocent II., who inquired of him particularly concerning Ireland, and who, before his departure, gave him special tokens of his favour, and appointed him legate in the place of Gilbert of Limerick, who now through old age and infirmity was no longer equal to the duties of the office.

Malachy placed his views before the Pope, and presented his schemes of reformation—chief amongst which was the establishment of a regular hierarchy under the control of the papal see: the Pope to send palls to the archbishops, thus at the same time asserting his authority and procuring from them an acknowledgment of the same. The Pope at once entered into his ideas, and agreed to raise the sees of Armagh and Cashel to metropolitan rank. 'With regard to the palls,' said the sovereign pontiff, 'it is well to act in a more solemn way. Having called together bishops, clergy and nobles of the land, you must hold a general council; and thus by the consent and common vote of all, send some honourable persons over to ask for the pall, and it shall be given you.'

On his way back from Rome, Malachy again visited Bernard, and arranged that some young men from Ireland should be received at Clairvaux, and after having spent some time there, should return to their own country with others from the same convent, and establish a branch of the Cistertian order. The result of this was that in 1142, the abbey of Mellifont, near Drogheda, was founded. Shortly afterwards several other branches of the same order were planted in different places. The influence of these Cistertian monks did more than anything else to hasten the Romanizing of the Church of Ireland.

We have so often spoken of the monastic institutions of the Irish Church, that one might readily fall into the mistake of supposing that we have here nothing more than the mere bringing in of a new order of monks, who were to take their place side by side with those already in the country. But we must remember that the same name is often given to things that differ most materially. We speak of the constitution of the ancient Irish Church as 'monastic,' and we speak of the establishment at Mellifont as 'monastic'; we use the same name, but the two systems had scarcely any resemblance. The Irish Christian 'families,' busied with the cultivation of the ground, with the work of education and the arts of civilization, had nothing in common with the cloisters where men were bound with the vows of poverty, chastity, and obedience. Malachy and Bernard knew well that the two things were quite different, for the one says of his countrymen that they might have heard of the name, but had never actually seen a monk; and the other asserts that Ireland never had any experience in monastic religion.

The Cistertians thus imported into the country were zealous propagandists. Like all enthusiasts, they were narrow-minded, and could see no merit in anything beyond their own system. They therefore toiled incessantly, and laboured in season and out of season for what they deemed to be the reformation of the Church.

Agreeably to the Pope's instructions, Malachy assembled a synod for the purpose of sending a formal request to Rome that the pall should be bestowed on the Irish archbishops. But for some unexplained reason several years were allowed to elapse before this was done. In the meantime, besides establishing branches of the Cistertian order, he endeavoured to obtain the election of his own supporters whenever a see became vacant. In this way he secured that the bishops of Clogher and Cork, as well as the three Danish bishops and the Archbishop of Armagh, should be supporters of his policy and ready to second him in anything that he would propose. The synod was at length held at Holmpatrick in the year 1148. It is worthy of note that this place, which has now reverted to its old Irish name of Skerries, was within the Danish kingdom of Dublin. This fact, together with the long delay and the fact that the synod was a small one, would lead us to suppose that the project which he had in mind was one that did not commend itself to the majority of the people. There are few things, however, that cannot be carried in a popular assembly when a small band know exactly what they want, and work together in order to obtain it. The synod accordingly agreed to ask for the palls, and Malachy himself undertook to go to France, where the Pope was at the time, and present the petition in person. Death came to him before he could accomplish his mission. He had gone as far as the monastery at Clairvaux, but found that the Pope had returned to Italy. While waiting there, intending shortly to pursue his journey, he was taken with fever, and after a few days breathed his last in the place where above all others he would have wished to die.

The petition which he had intended to present to the Pope was taken in hand by the Cistertians, who forwarded it in due course to Rome—the result being that after a time Paparo, a cardinal, was deputed to visit Ireland, and bestow the palls that had been desired. He arrived towards the end of the year 1151, and spent some time in the country. He remained a week at Armagh, and probably visited some other of the bishops. Early in the following year arrangements were made for the holding of a synod, which actually met at Kells on the 9th of March. The place was well chosen, as Kells was the site of an important Columban monastery, and it might disarm opposition to have the meeting held at a centre where all the associations were purely Irish. But the whole business of the assembly was managed by the foreign monks of Mellifont, and the synod was regarded with suspicion by many of the native Irish. The Columban party stayed away. Even the Bishop of Kells kept aloof, and several others were conspicuous by their absence.

As soon as the proceedings opened, it was made manifest that this synod was to be different from any ever held before in Ireland. Formerly, when laity and clergy met, it was to take counsel, and decide by a majority of votes what was for the good of the Church. Now it appeared that they were merely assembled to receive the commands of their ruler. At Holmpatrick they had asked for two palls—one for Armagh and the other for Cashel. The Pope, however, was swayed by other influences, and had already decided that four were to be bestowed. Dublin and Tuam were also to have archiepiscopal rank, and thus the Danish see, which had been only a few years in existence, and had never been in communion with the Church of Ireland, was put on a level with places which had historic associations and had grown with the Church's growth. Some of the clergy were indignant, specially those of Armagh and Down. An old Irish account tells us that 'it was in violation of the rights of the clergy of Patrick and Columkill that the pall was given to the church of Dublin, or even to that of Tuam.'[1] But it was too late now for such protests. When the Coarb of Patrick was only third—an Italian priest (Cardinal Paparo) and a Danish bishop (Christian, of Waterford, papal legate) taking precedence before him—when no place at all was found for the Coarb of Columkill—when French Cistertians were masters of the ceremonies, and Irish abbots were barely tolerated: there was no place left for the assertion of Irish independence. As a free and national institution, the Irish Church ceased to exist at the Synod of Kells.

[1] *Book of Flann MacEogan*, quoted by Bp. Reeves. *Antiquities of Down, Connor and Dromore*, p. 141.

CHAPTER XIX.

THE ANGLO-NORMAN INVASION.

THE decrees of the Synod of Kells were followed up by other measures which had the same end in view: the bringing of the Church of Ireland into conformity with the Church of England and of Rome. At a synod held at Clane, on the Liffey, it was enacted that the teachers in all the ecclesiastical schools should receive their education at Armagh. This, if it could have been carried out, would have been the most efficacious method of all. Then the Cistertians extended themselves, and soon six large establishments were in connection with the order in Ireland. But all this might have had but little effect were it not for an event—the most momentous in Irish history—which happened shortly after, and which completed the work of bringing Ireland under the power of the Pope. I mean the Anglo-Norman conquest.

Early in the reign of Henry II. of England, the king had turned his attention to the conquest of the neighbouring island. A plausible pretext for thus attacking a perfectly independent state presented itself in the slave trade which the Irish had long carried on, buying the children of needy Englishmen, and disposing of them in different parts of Ireland. As further justification there was the religious one, that Ireland alone of Western nations was not subject to the see of Rome, and that, according to the current ideas of that time, the position of her Church was schismatical and heretical.

Henry, though not overburdened with religion, was fully alive to the advantage of the Church's sanction. It was by the interposition of the Church that he had been raised to the throne; for it was the Archbishop of Canterbury who arranged the terms of the Treaty of Wallingford, whereby it was agreed that Stephen was to hold the throne for his life, but the succession was to be secured to Henry. A trusty messenger, therefore, laid his designs concerning Ireland before the Pope, who, by a strange coincidence, happened to be the first and last Englishman that ever occupied the papal chair. The result was that a Bull was issued authorizing the conquest, recognizing that to subjugate Ireland would be to 'widen the boundaries of the Church,' claiming that Ireland belongs of right to the Holy See, simply because it is an island, and reserving an annual tribute of one penny for every house in the country.

No sooner had this Bull been received than Henry brought the subject forward at the Council of Winchester, proposing that an expedition should set out, and that the kingdom should be conquered and handed over to his brother, William of Anjou. The opposition which the king received caused him to relinquish the project for a time; and soon other concerns so fully occupied his attention that it seemed as if the authorization he had obtained would never be utilized.

At length an opportunity presented itself, arising from the disputes among the Irish leaders themselves. Dermot, King of Leinster, had drawn upon himself the enmity of Tiernan, Prince of Breffni. The chief King of Ireland took up the prince's quarrel, and in the battle that ensued Dermot was defeated and had to fly for his life. He made his way to England, and thence to France, presented himself before the King of England, and obtained his sanction to raise what forces he could among the king's subjects.

The story of the conquest of Ireland is one that belongs to the secular history, and need not here be repeated. We have only to consider its influence on the religious condition of the country. On the English side the conquest was regarded as a holy war. The Irish were enemies to the Church, and were to be subdued in order to bring them to obedience. The papal blessing was bestowed on the project from the first. Not only did Pope Adrian issue the Bull to which reference has been already made, but his successor, Alexander III., followed it up with a confirmatory Bull, and wrote letters on the subject to nearly all the parties concerned. In a letter of this latter prelate, he accuses the Irish of the crimes of incest and concubinage; but he somewhat weakens the force of his rebuke by coupling with them, as crimes of equal enormity, that they eat meat in Lent, and pay no tithes. In another letter he says, that 'our dearly beloved son in Christ, the illustrious Henry King of England,' undertook the subjugation of Ireland, because 'he was pressed in his conscience by the voice of a Divine inspiration.' The whole expedition, therefore, was undertaken under cover of religion, and had for one of its professed objects the subjugation of the Irish Church.

One of the first acts of Henry in Ireland was to assemble those of the ecclesiastics who were willing to answer his summons. The bishops answered with alacrity. We have already seen that the dominant party amongst them consisted of men who were either foreigners or Irishmen brought up under foreign influence, and who, like Malachy, 'drew no more from the country of their birth than the fishes of the sea draw from their native element.' Their sympathies were with Henry more than with any Irish ruler. Answering to the king's summons, they assembled in synod at Cashel in 1172, and passed enactments decreeing uniformity between the Irish and the English Churches.

Only one thing remained to be done. It was to destroy those establishments where the old Irish monastic system remained still in force. According to the Romish view, these places were well described by Pope Adrian as 'nurseries of vice.' They kept alive a spirit of opposition to the innovations of the new-comers; and they had with them the hearts of the people—a thing in which the new-comers had to a great extent failed. As long as they remained, the decrees of synods were made only to be broken.

If Henry had been able to establish a vigorous control over the whole of the island, this work could have been easily and promptly accomplished. But the English over-lordship was for a long time only a moderate extension of the old Danish settlements. The allegiance rendered by the native kings who swore fealty to the English sovereign, was very like the allegiance which in former times they gave to their own ardrigh or chief king; that is to say, it was a variable, and often a negative quantity. Within certain circumscribed limits English law reigned supreme, and in these districts the native establishments were ruthlessly destroyed. New monasteries were founded on the ancient sites, and in some places it was made a rule that no Irishman should for the future be admitted as an inmate. These proceedings caused bitter hatred on the part of the natives, but the new rulers utterly disregarded them.

A tragic story is told of Hugh de Lacy, to whom was given the lordship of Meath. He was the founder of many monasteries, which he richly endowed with wealth that was not his own. In founding these he destroyed many of the old Irish establishments. Amongst other places, he built an abbey at Durrow, in the King's County, and before doing so dispersed one of the oldest and most important of the Columban communities. He also erected a castle at the same place. One day while he was superintending the erection of the new buildings, a young man suddenly rushed upon him, severed his head from his body with one blow of his axe, and before the bystanders had recovered from their surprise he had made his escape to the friendly Irish, by whom he was sheltered and regarded as a hero. 'This was in revenge of Columkill,' is the remark made by the Annalists. They tell us, too, that De Lacy was 'the profaner and destroyer of many churches.' The foreign monasteries thought differently. The monks of St. Thomas, Dublin, contended with the Cistertians of Bective for the honour of obtaining De Lacy's body, just as if his relics were the relics of a saint. The authority of the Pope had to be invoked for the settlement of the dispute.

In the more remote parts of the country, where English authority did not extend, the case was different. There the old Irish customs still prevailed, and the people clung to the traditions of their fathers. But the cause was a failing one. The new *régime* had everything in its favour. The old system had lost its vitality, and only showed the last gasps of a life the vigour of which belonged to another age.

For the most part the English Church party treated the Irish with the bitterest hostility. But its friendship was still more to be dreaded. An Irish abbot or bishop who accepted any rank from the new-comers gave up at once his independence, and by the very act made himself subject to the Pope. And when it suited their purpose they could change their hostility to friendliness.

We have an example in the case of Flaherty O'Brolcan, a contemporary of Gelasius of Armagh. He was Abbot of Derry, and became the leader of the Columban party in Ireland. Under his vigorous rule there was a partial resuscitation of the old life of the order. But it held quite aloof from the innovating movements, and was therefore for the most part ignored by the Danish and English party. An effort was, however, made to identify Flaherty with the Romanizers. A synod was held near Trim in 1158. The papal legate was present, with bishops and clergy, but the laity were excluded. This was in itself characteristic of the new methods, for the Irish synods always admitted the laity. Here Flaherty was given rank, like the other bishops, and the special dignity of Arch-abbot of Ireland was invented for him. But they were only partially successful in securing his adhesion, and so we hear no more mention of the arch-abbacy.

CHAPTER XX.

CONCLUSION.

LITTLE more remains to be said. We have seen that the two parties continued for a time to exist side by side. Envy, bitterness and bigotry remained long after every other distinction had passed away. Strange as it may seem, the enmity between Protestants and Roman Catholics, which is still characteristic of some parts of the country, is historically connected with this bitterness of feeling which once existed between the Irish and the Romish Church.

If we are to pay attention to the foreign sources of information which have come down to us, we must believe that the Irish Church had sunk so low that there was nothing to regret in its final extinction. Immorality and incest are said to have been openly practised in the land; and it must be admitted that several authorities bear the same testimony. Nothing in the native sources of information, however, would lead us to conclude that there was the least truth in the charge. It is admitted, too, on all hands that it was a question of morality which first gave the Anglo-Normans a footing in Ireland, and that it was they who supported the adulterer, and not the Irish. There is also reason to suspect that all the authorities who charge the Irish with immoral practices derived their information from the same source, and that they represent, therefore, not many testimonies, but only one, and that one most unfriendly and unjust to the Irish. Surely, then, we may allow that the charge labours under considerable doubt, and is certainly very much exaggerated.

A further charge has also been made that the Irish had become uncivilized and barbarous. With regard to this, it is no doubt true that in backward places there were then, as now, some who were not abreast with the progress of the age. But that the charge is otherwise without foundation is shown by the clearest of all arguments. A few of the works of that age have escaped the destroyer, and remain to the present. In buildings, there are the round towers and the stone-roofed oratories; in stonework, there are the sculptured crosses; in metal, there are the various shrines, book-covers and croziers. These all display an originality and ability far removed from barbarism. The next age swept most of such things away, and brought in nothing to take their place. There is not one ancient Irish work of illuminating, sculpture, or metal-working which does not date from before the time when the Church of Ireland was made subject to the Church of Rome.

One cannot help regretting that no reformer was raised up by God to bring into order those things which had become disordered, at the same time retaining the independence of the Church. But God's ways with communities, as with individuals, are past finding out. Perhaps there is still some work reserved for the Irish Church. Once she held aloft the lamp of truth, and was a shining light to all Western Europe. The Lord may again choose her for the accomplishment of His high and holy purposes. When that call comes, God grant that she may be ready!

INDEX.

Abbots, 46; how elected, 68.

Abyssinia, founding of Church of, 13.

Adamnan, Abbot of Iona, *Life of St. Columba*, 59; visits Saxonland, 137; adopts and advocates Roman Easter, *ib.*; banished from Iona, *ib.*

Adrian, Pope, Bull of, 182.

Aidan, Saint, 91, 114.

Alexander III., Bull of, 183.

Anchorites, 84, *sq.*; not in earliest times, 88; enclosed, 86.

Anmchara or soul friend, 101; an adviser, not a confessor, *ib.*; resemblance to Old Testament prophets, 103.

Archbishop, title given to those who were not Metropolitans, 140.

Ardrigh, 28.

Armagh, rises to prominence in eighth century, 134; Book of, 138; influence of, on Romish side, 139; contest as to the abbacy of, 149, *sq.*; rule extended to Connaught, etc., 149, 150.

Augustine, Saint, of Canterbury, his work confined to south of England, 110; overtures to the British Church, 111; meets the British delegates, 112; curious test as to his character, 112.

Baithen, Abbot of Iona, 65.

Bede, 8.

Bega, or, Bees, Saint, 96.

Bernard of Clairvaux, Saint, *Life of Malachy*, 8, 170; his description of the Irish Church, 171.

Bishops, position of, 46; great numbers of, *ib.*; fighting, 139.

Boromean tribute, 105.

Bridget, Saint, 91; bishops subject to, 92.

Brie, Saint Fara's monastery at, 95.

British and Irish Churches alike in doctrine, 112.

Brude, King of the Picts, 58.

Cædmon, 96.

Cashel, archbishopric of, 180; synod of, 184.

Celestius, 15.

Celibacy, 43, 122.
Cellach, Bishop of Armagh, 165.
Chad, Saint, ordination of, 121.
Churches, dedication of, 47.
Cistertian Order, introduction of, 177.
Clane, synod of, 181.
Clement and Albin, 130.
Coarb, 99.
Coldingham, 97.
Columba, or Columkill, Saint, birth of, 54; founder of Derry, *ib.*; dispute with Finnian, 56; leaves Ireland, 57; preaching of, 58; death of, 65.
Columbian Order, decline of, 131, 148.
Columbanus, to be distinguished from Columba, 70; meaning of name, 71, 72; writings of, 71; settles in Burgundy, 72; banished by Theodoric, 73; reform of monasticism, 74; rule of, 74, 75; letter to the French bishops, 77; to Pope Boniface, 77, 78; to Pope Gregory, 78; on the supremacy of Rome, 80.
Comgal, monastic school of, at Bangor, 71.
Confession and absolution, 104.
Cooldreeny, battle of, 56, 101.
Cormac of Cashel, 154.
Cormac Mac Art, 38.
Corman, Bishop, fails to evangelize the Saxons, 113.
Cummian, 128.
Curse, ecclesiastical, 106.

Danes, 141, *sq.*; invasions of, 141; not as formidable as in England, 142; attacked the monasteries, 144; first appearance of, *ib.*; not religious enthusiasts, 145; settlements of, 156; retained their connection with England, 157; conversion of, 158; their bishops ordained at Canterbury, 160.
Dermaid, King, remarkable decision of, 55.
Dermot, King of Leinster, 182.
Deserts in Irish monasteries, 85.
Destruction of British Christianity, 53.
Druidism, 29, 42.
Dublin, Archbishopric of, 180.

Easter controversy, 116, *sq.*, 126, *sq.*
Easter fires, 29.
Eastern monasticism, Irish resemblances to, 41; differences, 42.
Economist, 100.
Erenach, 100.

Family, ecclesiastical, 100.
Felim, Bishop and King of Cashel, 153.
Fintan, visit to Iona, 101.

Gall, Saint, 73.
Gelasius of Armagh, 169.
Georgia, founding of the Church of, 13.
Gilbert, first papal legate in Ireland, 161, 166.

Gildas, 83.
Giraldus Cambrensis, 8.
Gregory, Pope, sends Augustine to England, 110.

Henry II., King of England, 181.
Hereditary succession in Irish bishoprics, 162.
Hilda, Saint, 95.
Holmpatrick, synod of, 178.
Honorius, Pope, letter of, 127.
Hugh de Lacy, death of, 185.

Immorality, charged against Irish Church, 187.
Iona, 58, 60, *sq.*, 135; decline of, 136; attacked by Danes, 145.
Isolation of Irish Church, 53; increased by Saxon invasion of England, *ib.*
Island of Saints, 50.

Justin Martyr, 11.
Jewish rites in Irish Church, 67.

Kells, the new Iona, 145; synod of, 179, *sq.*
Kildare, 91; illumination of manuscripts at, 93; sacred fire of, *ib.*

Learning in Irish monasteries, 71.
Lindisfarne, 114.

Maelsuthain, soul friend to Brian Boru, 103.
Malachy, Saint, appointed Bishop of Armagh, 167; ejected, 168; Life of, by St. Bernard, 8, 170; visits Rome, 176; death of, 179.
Mansuetus, 15.
Manuscripts, illuminated, 64.
Mellifont, 177.
Molaise, soul friend to Columba, 57.
Monastery, Irish, described, 40; for both sexes, 44, 95.
Monastic system of Irish Church, 14, 38, 66; origin of, 38; disadvantages of, 50; differs from modern monasticism, 177.
Monastic Rules, lax and strict, 83.

Needfire, 29.
Norsemen, not evangelized until a late period, 13.

O'Brolcan, Flaherty, 186.
Ordinations, difference of, between Rome and Ireland, 120; of Irish not admitted by Rome, 147.
Oswald, King of Northumbria, 113.

Palladius, 116.
Palls for Irish Archbishops, 176.
Paparo, Cardinal, visits Ireland, 179.
Paschal Controversy, 77. *See* Easter.
Patrick, Saint, captivity in Ireland, 17; writings of, 18; life in Britain, 22; biographies of, 8, 23, 139; connection with Gaul, 21; sup-

posed mission from Rome, 24, 25; preaching of, 26; *Breastplate*, 34; evangelical doctrine preached by, 36; 'family' of, 47.

Picts, missions to, 54.

Prosper of Aquitaine, 15.

Saints, three classes of, 44.

Samthann, abbess, 94.

Scotland, name of, 57.

Scribes in eighth century, 131.

Scriptures, Celtic revision of, 132; vernacular translation of, 133; esteemed by the Irish, 134.

Secularization of the Church, 152.

Senan, Saint, 90.

Soul-friend, *see* Anmchara.

Supremacy of the pope rejected, 115.

Tara, 29; desertion of, 107.

Teaching of Irish Church, 66.

Teltown, synod of, 56.

Tonsure, 119, *sq.*

Transubstantiation, 173.

Tribal system, 27, 45, 56.

Trim, synod of, 186.

Tuam, archbishopric of, 180.

Turgesius, 142.

Virgil the Geometer, 131.

William the Conqueror, 159.

Women, ministry of, 89, *sq.*; Columba's objection to, 89.

www.ingramcontent.com/pod-product-compliance
Lightning Source LLC
Chambersburg PA
CBHW020237170426
43202CB00008B/123